NOW
YOU WILL
EXCUSE
ME

NOW YOU WILL EXCUSE ME

Bite-Sized Lessons for the Leader in All of Us

JIM O'BRIEN

Writers of the Round Table Press
PO Box 1603, Deerfield, IL 60015
www.roundtablecompanies.com

Printed in the United States of America

First Edition: April 2020
10 9 8 7 6 5 4 3 2 1

Library of Congress Cataloging-in-Publication Data
O'Brien, Jim.
Now you will excuse me: bite-sized lessons for the leader in
all of us / Jim O'Brien.—1st ed. p. cm.
ISBN Paperback: 978-1-61066-080-8
ISBN Digital: 978-1-61066-081-5
Library of Congress Control Number: 2020902890

Writers of the Round Table Press and the logo
are trademarks of Writers of the Round Table, Inc.

Lead Editor: **James Cook**
Cover Designer: **Christy Bui**
Illustrator: **Christy Bui**
Interior Designer: **Sunny DiMartino**
Proofreaders: **Adam Lawrence, Carly Cohen**

For Michelle.

"Giorraíonn beirt bóthar."

Gaelic saying, meaning "Two shorten the road."[1]

---

1   James O'Donnell, *Classic Irish Proverbs: In English and Irish*, (San Francisco: Chronicle Books, 1998), p. 75.

Contents

Foreword   xi
Introduction   xvii

Part I   The Wisdom of Others

2   Rising Orion and the Stolen Five Dollars
7   The Way of Rhythm
11   Learning to See
15   Having a Foot Fetish
19   My Dad, the "Mad Man"
22   My First Leadership Advice: TANSTAAFL
25   What's Your Timing?
28   One Driveway Equals Ninety-Four
     Chocolate-Covered Pretzels
31   Lessons from the Book of Dad
34   Cigar-Butt Leadership
37   Don't Go There
40   My One-Person Chain Gang
44   When Things Fall Apart
48   Doing What I Was Born For
51   Loving Our Fate
54   Sorcerers and Stupidity
57   Mission First or People Always?
60   Mr. Remainder
64   Samurai Rules
67   Samurai Rules: Part Two
70   Samurai Rules: Part Three
73   "Florida Has Been Very, Very Good to Me"

Part II Lessons Learned from Running

79   Endure vs. Embrace
82   Staring at Our Fears
85   Local Knowledge
89   University of Ultramarathon: Six Business
     Lessons from Running One Hundred Miles
96   Tight Looseness
99   The Most Persistent Question
103 Running Your Own Race
105 Lessons Learned from My Personal Worst
109 When Less Is More
112 Going the Extra Mile (for the Wrong Reasons)
116 My Own Personal Superpower
119 The Last, Best Day

Part III Finding Inspiration in Nature

125 What Am I Missing?
129 Not a Hero, Not a Zero
133 Go Slow and Make Things
136 Getting Growth Just Right
138 Indigos and Intuition
141 What's Your Weediness?

Part IV Personal Reflections

146 From White Belt to Black Belt to White Belt Again
150 The Dawn Patrol
153 Lazy and Cutthroat
157 Cowboy Jim
160 I Was Just Trying to Help
163 I Was Just Trying to Help: Part Two
168 Solitaire Leadership
172 Me vs. Me
176 Chasing the Sale
179 Sunk-Cost Bias: My Three-Year Mistake

183 Going into Debt

186 Getting Out of My Own Way

189 Self-Interest or Self-Delusion? The Eternal
     Challenge of Leadership

192 My Own Personal Blindside

196 Loving Being Wrong

199 James and the Baby Unicorn

202 Authentic or Auto-Tune?

205 Your Favorite Banned Songs

208 What I Learned at My Ninety-Day Off-Site

211 Going Stale

214 Seeing the Small Things

217 Getting Out of the Way

220 Tickets and Triggers

223 Solo Jumping

226 Comfortably Numb

230 Squirrel!

233 Ego, Anger, and Road Rage

236 The Toughest Puzzle

239 One Thing Every Leader Should Do

241 Taking Shortcuts

244 Embracing the Suck

246 It's Always about Me. It's Never about Me.

249 Last-Place Hero

Conclusion   **253**

Acknowledgments   **255**

About the Author   **257**

Foreword

Creators are lifelong learners. Jim O'Brien is clearly both a creator and lifelong learner.

I am honored that Jim asked me to write this foreword. Jim and I connected through the internet as a result of his learning about my TED* (*The Empowerment Dynamic)® work through his participation in the Stagen Leadership Academy. The core of TED* is making the shift from the roles of Victim, Persecutor, and Rescuer that make up the Dreaded Drama Triangle (DDT) to the empowering and resourceful roles of Creator, Challenger, and Coach that comprise TED roles that Jim attempts to model in his life and book.

David Brooks—my favorite columnist—wrote in one of his *New York Times* columns about visiting the Kansas Leadership Center and observing their mantra that "Leadership is an activity, not a position. Anyone can lead, anytime, anywhere."[1] Jim reflects this mantra in his writings.

This wonderful book of essays, reflections, and lessons learned about life and leadership is for anyone

---

1   David Brooks, "The Meritocracy is Ripping America Apart," *New York Times*, September 12, 2019, https://www.nytimes.com/2019/09/12 /opinion/markovits-meritocracy.html.

who embraces their Creator essence and leadership in life, which is . . . everyone.

Jim himself has achieved much by expressing his leadership in hundreds of diverse ways, both in organizations and in his life.

As I read his essays on lessons learned, I could not help but recall the Center for Creative Leadership (CCL) book *The Lessons of Experience*, which was instrumental early in my career in leadership development.[2] CCL found that successful executives were "ready to grab or create opportunities for growth, wise enough to not believe there's nothing more to learn, and courageous enough to look inside themselves and grapple with their frailties."[3]

By any measure, Jim is such a successful executive, as is perhaps best exemplified when he writes, "I am writing not as a knower or a wise man but as a person searching for answers about how to be a better leader. My quest will go on until I die, and in the meantime, I wanted to set down what I have learned."

In fulfilling his sense of purpose and calling in writing this book, he uses humor and humility, a compelling light touch that is never "preachy."

In addition to conveying the lessons he learned as an executive and consultant, Jim also distills the wisdom of others here: maxims from Stoics, samurai, sensei, and Zen masters; inspiration and insight from nature; integrated learning from the Stagen Leadership

---

2   Morgan W. McCall Jr., Michael M. Lombardo, and Ann M. Morrison, *The Lessons of Experience: How Successful Executives Develop on the Job* (New York: Free Press, 1988).

3   Morgan W. McCall Jr., Michael M. Lombardo, and Ann M. Morrison, *The Lessons of Experience* (New York: The Free Press, 1988), p. 122.

Academy; precepts drawn from his voracious reading; principles gleaned from running; and much, much more. Most importantly, Jim shares the understanding that comes from tapping into his "inner observer."

Perhaps his most often referenced source of learning is his dad, to whom he refers to time and time again. Reading all the ways he learned from his dad made me reflect on my own father. So, if you will excuse me, I feel drawn to a dad diversion . . .

My dad was a traveling salesman, covering a three-state area in the Midwest by car. In all those years and on all those cars he went through, he had one—and only one—bumper sticker: "Courtesy is Contagious."

He adopted that motto in his life—and mine.

Late at night on weekends, when I would return from running around with friends and/or girlfriends, Dad and I would often have long conversations about issues of the day and about life in general. One time I said to him, "Gee, Dad, you seem to have it all figured out!"

After a deep belly laugh, he replied, "David, the older I get, the more I realize how much I don't know."

Another maxim of Dad's was, "The key to a life well-lived is that you leave the world a better place as a result of your having been here."

I share these memories not to shift the focus to Dad and me, but to say that these are the kinds of memories and reflections that will emerge for you as you read these essays. Also, with the writing of this book, Jim O'Brien has fulfilled my dad's principle of leaving the world a better place.

His experiences are not all "goodness and light." When facing obstacles and setbacks, he never describes himself as a Victim of circumstance (which indeed are sometimes circumstances of his own making) and never calls the people who block his way or cause him pain Persecutors. Instead, he reflects on these events and people as Challengers that call forth learning and growth.

As he concludes, "Our journey as leaders is to keep evolving and growing so we can meet the challenges we face on a daily basis." Again, we are ALL leaders—and Creators—on this journey.

Finally, here is my suggestion on how to engage with this book.

First, read the whole book.

Next, commit to a practice of reading one essay per week, and observe your own experience that week through the lens of Jim's lesson learned. That will provide you with a year and a half of "slow-drip" learning and integration.

—**David Emerald Womeldorff**, cofounder of the Bainbridge Leadership Center, and author of *The Power of TED** (**The Empowerment Dynamic*), *3 Vital Questions: Transforming Workplace Drama*, and the forthcoming *Seven Commitments for Conscious Collaboration*
www.PowerofTED.com
www.3VitalQuestions.com

Fellow survivors
Winter weary
The old pickup and I
Sputter in the spring sun

Introduction

My journey into leadership has been one of fits and starts. This book details some of those fits and starts, and reflects on what I learned along the way, both good and bad.

I have always been afraid of being found out as an impostor who didn't belong in whatever role I was in. Whether it was managing an IT department, overseeing a portfolio of shopping malls, or running the US business for a British investment manager, I was always afraid. I had good reason to be afraid. In every instance, I had little idea what I was doing. But I was willing to learn. I looked for the answers in books, in the examples of others, in running, and even in nature. Sometimes I found the answers, and sometimes I didn't. This book is for my fellow impostors, who are also looking for their answers. While I don't have all the answers, I hope this book provides some comfort that you are not alone. I also hope you can profit from learning about my mistakes and avoiding them yourself.

This book explores my journey into leadership. My favorite samurai, Miyamoto Musashi, once said that when you know "The Way"—you see it in all things. I think he was right, and I continually see The Way of leadership in all things: what to do, what not to do, my mistakes, the mistakes of others, what works, what doesn't work. Every day I see something that makes me think about how it applies to leadership.

Beginning with the Hardy Boys, I have read hundreds of mystery novels. But in the last few years, my appetite for these types of novels has waned as I discovered a richer set of mysteries: people. We are complex, complicated, and contradictory creatures. There is no greater mystery to solve than understanding other people as well as us. My journey into leadership has been like that of a detective trying to solve a case, looking for clues, going down rabbit holes, and sometimes having insights. Many of these insights were about understanding others and myself. The book is a map of my journey as I looked for clues in the works of the Stoics, within running and martial arts, in nature, and in the lessons I learned from my parents.

My former colleague Chuck Thompson, a talented musician, once told me about having a composition in his head and being unable to get it down on paper. Writing this book has been a bit like that: I haven't been able to quite get everything down or say I everything I have to say. And I am still very much on the journey with many more mysteries to ponder and solve.

At this point in my journey, I am willing to be more vulnerable and acknowledge my impostor-driven fears. While I will always have more to learn, I have grown more comfortable with the idea that I don't have it all figured out and never will. I hope this book will help you on your own journey, and I hope we meet along the way. And now you will excuse me while I start working on the next book . . .

Part I

THE WISDOM OF OTHERS

Rising Orion and the Stolen Five Dollars

In the middle of the night, I got up to go to the bathroom. When I came back to bed, my wife, Michelle, said, "Look, do you see Orion?"

In that sleepy, middle-of-the-night moment, I went back in time—back to being a small boy—and remembered Grandma Louise.

My Grandma Louise lived in Hollywood, Florida. I didn't know much about Florida back then. I knew it had palm trees and pink flamingos and alligators and Grandma Louise. My siblings and I would occasionally receive presents through the mail from Grandma Louise. It was always exciting to receive a big brown box with a Florida postmark; we knew it had to be from her. Once she sent us squirt guns shaped like alligators, and I couldn't have been more thrilled. After that, I always kept an eye out for the postman to see if he was bringing another package from Florida.

One week a card arrived from Grandma Louise. Rather than sending us gifts, she had sent a check for thirty-five dollars. The thirty-five dollars represented five dollars apiece for my siblings and me. Five dollars!

It was all the money in the world to me. I could buy enough candy for the rest of my life and probably have money left over for toys. I couldn't wait to get my five dollars.

Shortly after the check from Grandma Louise arrived, Dad came home from work carrying a big box from Sears.

"What's that, Dad?" we all said.

"It's a telescope!" Dad said. "I used the check from Grandma Louise to buy a telescope."

It took me a few more questions to work out that Dad had used all our money, my money, to buy the telescope. I couldn't believe it.

I didn't want a telescope . . . I wanted my five dollars.

Dad explained how great the telescope was and how we could use it to look at the stars and the moon. It slowly became clear to me that the telescope was Dad's. He wanted to look at the universe and had used Grandma Louise's check to get his telescope. Worse still, it wasn't to be used for looking at birds or planes or across the street. It was for looking at the moon and the stars.

Boring!

In the evening, Dad would get out the telescope and look at stars or the moon and invite us to peer through the telescope and see what he was seeing. The best nights for looking at the universe were cold, crisp nights during winter. Standing outside in the cold dark, waiting to see a twinkle had no appeal to me. Although Dad tried bribing me with hot chocolate when we went back inside, I didn't like hot chocolate, and after a while I simply refused to go outside.

Before I stopped going out in the dark, Dad tried teaching us some of the constellations. I only learned one of them, Orion the Hunter. I only learned Orion because for a while I thought it was called O'Brien, and it seemed cool that there was a constellation with the same name as me.

In the Northern Hemisphere, Orion is a winter constellation most easily seen from November through March. As I grew older, I came to have a love–hate relationship with Orion. On the one hand, Orion reminds me of childhood and Dad and Grandma Louise. On the other hand, he represents the long, dark nights of wintertime.

I had mostly forgotten about Orion after I became an adult. But one morning in August, I went out for a short run. I am not a morning person nor a morning runner, and I always feel creaky and ancient shuffling through the predawn darkness. I was feeling exactly this way when I hit the halfway point in the run. Pausing for a minute in the parking lot of a park, I stared up at the sky, looking at the stars. Up in the dark sky I saw Orion. How could that be? It was August, not December. After doing some research, I learned Orion begins to appear during the early morning at the end of the summer. As summer turns to fall, he appears sooner and sooner until winter, when he rises soon after sunset.

Since then, I have come to view the August sightings of Orion as another harbinger of fall, like seeing the first aster flowers that wink on during August, and the cottonwood leaves that begin falling as school starts. August Orion reminds me of the rhythm of the world and how it keeps turning with or without us. Like him or not, Orion will appear every August and signal winter is coming.

Like Orion, leadership goes on forever. I wrote this book to pass along the things I have learned about being a leader.

While I have had many wonderful teachers and mentors, some of my leadership journey has been trial and error, and I hope the reader can learn from my experiences.

I have had a career as a generalist, working in real estate and investment management. I had no training for these areas, and learned as I went along. Consequently, I made even more mistakes than the average person, and I am grateful for the patience and kindness of my colleagues, who helped me in so many instances. Being a generalist has been the right place for me as it taps into my love of learning and offers constant and varied challenges, some of which feature in this book.

I am writing not as a knower or a wise man but as a person searching for answers about how to be a better leader. My quest will go on until I die, and in the meantime I wanted to set down what I have learned.

We are here on this earth just a short while and have even less time as leaders. We never know how people will remember us, or for what. Was it our brilliant insight in the Monday morning meeting? Probably not. Or was it doing something to show you cared about your team? Maybe. Was it teaching someone something? Perhaps. But if you take the time to teach and to care during your time as a leader, it's possible sometime, decades from now, that someone will remember and smile as they sleepily look up at the night sky.

And now you will excuse me; I have to go search for alligator squirt guns on eBay . . .

The Way
of Rhythm

There is a new hole in the September sky. It was once filled with swallows who left suddenly, called by a hum in the earth I cannot hear. Only when I noticed the sky was different did I realize the swallows had departed overnight. For me, the swallows embody summer as they dart back and forth eating insects. While they are here, I sometimes pause to watch them, and through them I savor the wonder and beauty that is summer in the Midwest. The empty sky now makes it impossible for me to ignore fall's coming arrival.

I have been thinking about rhythm a lot lately. I first became aware of rhythm as something to pay attention to while reading the *The Five Rings* by the samurai Miyamoto Musashi. Musashi writes, "In the career of a warrior, there is a rhythm to rising in service to one's master, and a rhythm to falling from favour, a rhythm to things going as expected, and a rhythm to the unexpected happening. Or, in the Way of Business, there is a rhythm to becoming wealthy, and a rhythm to wealth disappearing; in every Way there are different rhythms. In all things, the rhythms in which they thrive, and the rhythms in which they decline—you should carefully discern these."[1]

Musashi learned about rhythm while studying how to win a sword fight. In order to beat an opponent, he needed to understand his opponent's rhythm and respond with a different rhythm that his opponent would be unable to stop. Using his insights on rhythm and other skills, Musashi was 60–0 in duels.

Although we are not samurai fighting for our lives, rhythms are worth understanding because they inform every aspect of the world. Right now in my autumn garden, the air is filled with the constant motion of hummingbirds. They are preparing to migrate, alone, perhaps as far as twenty-seven hundred miles, and are gorging themselves for the long journey ahead. During September they are almost manic, hardly resting as they go from flower to flower. This is in sharp contrast to seeing them throughout the summer when they are more relaxed and feed less frequently.

Wherever we are, we are presented with countless rhythms. There are rhythms, as Musashi says, "in the Way of Business." People rising in service, and people falling from favor. There are the rhythms to meetings—how they begin and how they end. There are rhythms to reporting results, rhythms to board meetings, and rhythms to off-site meetings.

Understanding the rhythms of things helps us see things accurately. While visiting another company's office, I was ushered into a conference room, where

---

1   Miyamoto Musashi, *The Five Rings: Miyamoto Musashi's Art of Strategy*, translated by David K. Groff (New York: Chartwell Books, 2012), p. 73.

my arrival forced someone working on his laptop to leave. Apparently, there was no other space for him to work; the business was bursting at the seams. I sensed the rhythm of a thriving business. Later, someone hustled down the hall at a pace approaching a run. Again, I noted the rhythm of a thriving business full of drive to get things done. Finally, I heard someone having a conference call, his voice rising with tension. It was a good tension, without fear, and full of urgency about some unknown issue. In the short time I was in the conference room, I had been flooded with the rhythms of a company crackling with energy. I could feel the business pushing forward.

Just as there are rhythms of thriving, there are rhythms of decline. Shortly after joining a small firm, I began to see the rhythms of decline everywhere I looked. What did that look like? Lots of empty workstations, a lack of new clients, and a quiet, still workplace. There was no humming energy, just a few people quietly going about their work. While I didn't want to acknowledge these rhythms, when I reflected on them and compared them to the rhythms of a thriving business, it was obvious I needed to find another job.

Just as there are workplace rhythms, individuals also have their own rhythms. Some people are looking for advancement and dissatisfied with their job, while others are happy with their roles. Our challenge is in seeing all the various rhythms in our world. Sometimes all the rhythms are in harmony, and other times they are not, especially when the rhythms of the business meet the conflicting rhythms of individuals and teams.

There is no end to rhythms, and they are constantly changing like the seasons. When we see them accurately, we have the opportunity to act so that our people and business can thrive.

And now you will have to excuse me while I contact that company with the crackling energy about a job . . .

Learning to See

My friend Tom and I were catching up over drinks, and he told me about trying to help a friend seeking to change the industry he worked in. His friend was unhappy with his job and yearned to move into another industry where Tom has a lot of contacts. Always willing to be helpful, Tom agreed to introduce his friend to some of his key relationships in that industry.

Tom made the introductions by email, and a week went by without any response from his friend. Then a second week went by. After three weeks had passed, Tom called up his friend and asked whether he really wanted to change jobs and industries. His friend made some vague excuses, and Tom found their conversation frustrating. His friend had asked for his help, but when Tom gave him the help he was requesting, he failed to act. Later, Tom decided to stop trying to help his friend and apologized to his contacts for distracting them.

Tom's story illustrates something I call "watching the feet." Watching the feet means comparing what people say to what they actually do. In the case of Tom's friend, he said he wanted to change jobs and change industries. But when given the opportunity to connect with valuable employer contacts in his desired industry, he did nothing. His words said one thing, but his feet said another. His feet told the real story.

When we learn to watch the feet, we begin to see the world more clearly. We watch how well people's words line up with their deeds. When people's deeds are consistent with their words, all is good. There is nothing more for us to do beyond noting the other person is acting consistently with their words.

When people's deeds are inconsistent with their words, however, we receive valuable insights. In the case of Tom and his friend, Tom learned he was wasting his time and wisely gave up trying to be helpful.

Watching the feet is a tool leaders can use endlessly. My friend Kathy works for a large company. In the company's marketing materials, it describes at length their wonderful culture. However, when Kathy joined a culture committee dedicated to improving the company's culture, she found the committee had almost no budget. After her requests for additional budget monies were turned down, she confronted the senior management team at a town hall meeting. She described the gap between the company's words and its deeds in funding the culture committee. What Kathy was doing was watching her company's feet and calling out the inconsistency. As a result of Kathy's comments, the management team allocated more monies to the culture committee. In addition, Kathy now meets with a member of the senior management team to give him feedback on the company's culture.

Watching the feet is a useful tool for seeing the world more clearly. Often it helps us see blind spots, as was the case at Kathy's company.

Seeing our own blind spots is much more difficult, however. As recounted in *Ike's Bluff* by Evan Thomas, when Dwight Eisenhower was president, his staff dreaded when he turned up in the White House wearing a brown suit. His staff knew this meant he was in a bad mood. Eisenhower didn't know this, but his staff did. Eisenhower had a blind spot about how he dressed according to his mood.[2]

We all have blind spots.

While gathering feedback from a team about its organization and leaders, the staff told me how they were required to track their hours in order to bill clients. Although the team leader also billed her time to clients, she didn't track her time. The staff saw this as a classic example of two sets of rules—one for the boss, and one for everyone else. When we later spoke to the team leader about this, she hadn't realized how her behavior came off to the team. She had a blind spot when it came to tracking her time.

I, too, have my own blind spots. Someone who worked with me remarked on how often I looked at my phone during meetings. His feedback was that whenever I looked at my phone, I was sending a message to the other attendees that I wasn't listening, that my phone was more important than the people in the room, and that my attention was elsewhere. It was tough to hear this feedback, but it was a great insight about a blind spots.

---

2   Evan Thomas, *Ike's Bluff: President Eisenhower's Secret Battle to Save the World* (New York: Little, Brown and Company, 2012), p. 4.

Watching the feet is a useful tool for seeing others, but quite difficult to do when it comes to us. The way to learn about our blind spots is by asking for feedback. Three-hundred-and-sixty-degree feedback works well because it is anonymous and people will be candid in their remarks. Or you can pose questions such as, "What should I start doing? What should I stop doing? What should I continue doing?"

When you become aware of things to work on, measure them. In my case, tracking the number of times I picked up my phone in a meeting became a way to see myself more clearly.

Watching the feet is a powerful tool. When we apply it ourselves, it becomes a way to see ourselves as if in a mirror. And if you will now excuse me, I have to go to my closet and get rid of my brown suit . . .

Having a
Foot Fetish

In my last essay, I wrote about the idea of watching the feet and how it can be a powerful tool. At its most basic level, watching the feet means comparing what a person says to what they actually do. By comparing words to deeds, we can see inconsistencies and better understand another person. Watching words versus deeds is the most basic part of watching the feet, however. In this essay I will go deeper into the things we should be aware of as we watch the feet.

We should begin by accepting that people naturally seek to manipulate us. People bring us problems and tell us their side of the story. People come to us and speak well about themselves and speak poorly about others. Everyone has self-interest, and it is in his or her self-interest to convince you to see things their way. Understanding self-interest is a critical part of watching the feet. As Ben Franklin said, "Would you persuade? Speak of Interest, not of Reason."[3]

---

3   Benjamin Franklin, *Poor Richard's Almanack and Other Writings*, edited by Bob Blaisdell (Mineola, NY: Dover Publications, 2013), p. 50.

What Franklin meant was that self-interest is an extremely powerful motivator of our behavior. Therefore, to see things accurately and watch the feet, you must consider self-interest. What does the other person want? It is important to understand that what they want is often not what you want. Therefore, you have to understand your own self-interest, know what it is, and be prepared to compare your self-interest with the other person's. Over and over again, I have observed smart people making the mistake of assuming everyone else has the same self-interest as them and finding themselves blocked in achieving their goals as a result.

> One way to look for clues about self-interest is to observe body language.

In our highly connected world, where we are constantly peering at our phones, observing body language has nearly become a lost art. While attending a meeting of small-business CEOs, I heard a CEO named Bruce give an overview of his senior team. When Bruce began speaking about his long-term CFO, he took a chair and placed it in front of him, using it like a shield. When I asked him if he had an internal conflict regarding his CFO, Bruce confessed he wanted to fire him. He went on to say he was struggling to do so because he was conflict-averse and also felt a degree of loyalty to the CFO. It was the chair used as a shield that led me to probe and gain a deeper understanding of Bruce's issues.

Next time you are in a meeting, play a game with yourself, and turn off the sound of people's voices and closely watch their body language. In poker, body language observations are called "tells," and poker players work hard to disguise their tells. This rarely happens outside the poker table, however, and if you work on this, you will begin to observe many tells. Men, for example, often pull up their socks in preparation for a difficult conversation. Some people fiddle with a ring or a pen when they are stressed or nervous. Developing a laser-like concentration so you are fully present and observing tells is a helpful way to watch the feet. This is not to discount people's words or the sounds of their voice, but rather to emphasize that body language plus words give us a deeper understanding.

A subtle part of watching the feet includes observing the rhythm of things. There is rhythm to everything, including the rhythm of a workplace, the rhythm of a home, and the rhythm of an era. In our world of vibrations and dings and the seductive distraction of our phones, understanding rhythm takes work. I have worked in companies enjoying high growth, and their rhythms were far different from other companies that were shrinking. When we observe the rhythm of things, we can better watch the feet.

A great observer of rhythm is my former colleague, Chuck Thompson. Combining the business acumen of a seasoned executive with a degree in music composition, Chuck literally feels and hears rhythm in a way few people do. Using his rhythm insights, Chuck developed an unusually thoughtful set of mutual funds that continue to find strong demand with investors.

Understanding self-interest, body language, and rhythm are all part of watching the feet. These tools are available to us to better understand the world around us as well as ourselves. When we have a deep understanding of others and ourselves, we are more effective. And now you will excuse me while I go observe my self-interest . . .

My Dad, the "Mad Man"

Dad worked his entire career for a big insurance company in Chicago. During the 1960s, Dad went off to work dressed just like the people in the show *Mad Men*. He wore suits with narrow lapels and cuffed trousers, and carried a handkerchief. During summer he wore straw hats, and on frigid winter days he wore earmuffs under his fedora. He always wore highly polished cordovan wingtips, never black or brown.

During the week, Dad had a nighttime routine. Before going to bed, he would take out the shoes he would be wearing to work the next day and polish them. He had a wooden box that held his shoe polishing kit. In the box was Kiwi shoe polish, some rags, and a shoe brush. He would spread newspaper on the floor so that no shoe polish would stain the wood, spend five minutes polishing his shoes, and then go to bed. Lying in bed at night, I knew Dad would be going to bed soon when I heard the tin of the shoe polish open, followed by the rhythmic rustle of the rags applying the shoe polish.

As a kid, I felt something in Dad's routine. At one level it was a grown-up thing to do, because if you weren't careful, the shoe polish would stain or discolor the floor. But I felt something else, a feeling of tension perhaps. Of Dad being in the room but being elsewhere. And a feeling of putting on armor. Dad was getting ready for the next day, preparing himself. While he never talked about it, I feel sure the shoe polishing routine was part of examining what tomorrow would bring and making sure he was as ready as he could be.

Decades later, I now get it.

Preparation is one of the most valuable things we can do.

There are countless opportunities to prepare. For example, prior to meeting someone new, do you look at his or her LinkedIn profile and company bio? Do you make an effort to consider what you have in common or whom you both might know? For meetings, do you send out agendas in advance so that the attendees can be prepared?

While there is something challenging about winging it, I always find myself regretting it when I haven't prepared. A key cornerstone to David Allen's *Getting Things Done*[4] philosophy involves setting aside time each week to do what he calls a "weekly review." Part of doing the weekly review requires looking at the calendar for the upcoming week and asking if you are ready for the meetings on your calendar. It also means looking at the calendar for the week that just ended to make sure nothing has escaped your attention.

---

4   David Allen, *Getting Things Done: The Art of Stress-Free Productivity* (New York: Viking, 2001).

The weekly review is just one level of preparation. For meetings, it's useful to consider in advance what you and the other participants want to get out of the meeting. We are all self-centered at our core, so it's helpful to try and put yourself in the other attendees' shoes and consider what you would want if you were them. Often, it's very different from what you want. While it's impossible to always get this right, the very act of thinking about what the other person wants is helpful and makes us more effective.

While looking for a job, a firm asked me to give them some advice on selling one of their products. I decided to treat the meeting as a job interview and prepared deeply for the meeting. I read everything I could about the people I was meeting with, the company, and its products. I thought about their challenges and how I would approach solving them if I worked there. The meeting went well, and as a result of my preparation, I was offered a job at the company. It's unlikely this would have happened without the preparation I did in advance.

Preparation is not always fun. Like shining a pair of shoes, it can sometimes be tedious. Being prepared, however, is something within our control. Being prepared allows us to be focused and effective. And now you will have to excuse me; I have some cordovan wingtips to polish . . .

My First Leadership Advice: TANSTAAFL

I am from a family of seven children, and I am the oldest. Dad was also the oldest in his family, and he believed that the being the oldest carried certain responsibilities as well as benefits. One of the additional responsibilities was an expectation to set the example. If some of my siblings were misbehaving, it was my job to behave appropriately and demonstrate what they should be doing. If I chose to misbehave with them, I might find myself as the only one being punished, partially for not having set the example.

Dad also believed that being held to this higher standard brought benefits, including a special bond between him and me, as one oldest child to another. He sometimes said that because I was the oldest child, I was his favorite son. "Hello, Favorite Son," he might say when he entered the room I was in.

As a small boy, I excitedly told my Dad about a free offer I had seen on TV. I was very excited to get something for free. Dad listened to me and replied with one word: "TANSTAAFL."

To me, it sounded like Dad was saying, "Tan-Staff-Ul." Huh?

"What's 'TANSTAAFL,' Dad?"

"There Ain't No Such Thing as a Free Lunch."

I was initially baffled by what Dad meant. Later, I came to realize I was a living example of TANSTAAFL. I might be the favorite son, but the title came along with the expectation that I conduct myself to a higher standard than my siblings. No free lunch.

TANSTAAFL was the first piece of leadership advice I received, and one that stayed with me ever since. For me, it takes in the concept of "deliberate trade-offs," meaning that decisions often have difficult consequences that are hard to stomach. We should understand deliberate trade-offs and be willing to make tough decisions while managing the trade-offs.

Tough decisions are those decisions where no matter what the choice, there are consequences you would prefer to avoid but cannot. Sometimes those consequences impact us personally. For example, while in a senior role, I voted for a corporate transaction that would cost some of my colleagues and me our jobs. My boss Andrew referred to me as "the turkey who voted for Thanksgiving."

My decision was not taken lightly. I had months to consider the decision and its various trade-offs. If I found a way to kill the transaction, I would keep my job and so would my colleagues. Sooner or later, however, there would be a new transaction, and some or all of us would lose our jobs. By becoming a fierce protector of my team in the short term, I might be perceived as a blocker to the long-term growth of the business. If I were seen as a blocker, I would lose the ability to help my colleagues when the next transaction occurred.

In the end, I saw the transaction as the best thing for the firm, its shareholders, and my colleagues who kept their jobs. But there was no free lunch. The transaction meant some of us had to leave. When the day came to announce the deal to my team, I knew I had to set the example. I challenged them to see the transaction as an opportunity instead of an obstacle. Even for those of us losing our jobs, there were opportunities to learn new skills before we left (the transaction would take nine months to close) and to participate in a complicated merger that would add to our resumes.

For me, losing my job gave me the opportunity to embrace being a servant leader and help my colleagues during an awful time. Some people became angry or deeply depressed. Knowing I was losing my job gave me an opportunity to lead in a way I had never experienced. It gave me the opportunity to set the example.

I think of Dad's advice as "voice-in-my-head advice," something that resonated so deeply that it's like I'm actually hearing Dad's voice in my head. Even today, when faced with a tough decision, I can hear Dad's voice prompting me to consider the trade-offs and find the best way forward. And now you will please excuse me while I go get (a not free) lunch . . .

What's Your Timing?

The Japanese samurai Miyamoto Musashi was 60–0 in duels to the death. In his last duel, he fought a samurai named Sasaki Kojirō. As longtime rivals, Musashi and Kojirō had agreed that a duel was the only way to settle who the better swordsman was. According to most accounts, Musashi arrived at the duel two to three hours late. His late arrival angered Kojirō who flew into a rage. Attacking first, he narrowly missed Musashi who then killed Kojirō.

The duel illustrates two of the three types of timing in the martial arts: early timing and late timing (the third is same timing, which I won't discuss here). Early timing means striking at your opponent first, and late timing means waiting for your opponent's move and then, while evading it, striking at him or her.

In the case of the duel, Musashi used late timing first as a strategy and then as a tactic. By deliberately arriving late, Musashi made Kojirō anxious as well as angry. Musashi then used late timing to respond to Kojirō's initial strike. Kojirō, on the other hand, used early timing in attacking Musashi first. Perhaps if he had not been so angry, his early timing might have been successful. While some martial artists favor one type of timing over another, each instance is unique and no single timing is always appropriate.

The concept of timing has unlimited application in life and leadership. We can employ timing when making strategic decisions as well as having difficult conversations.

As we consider difficult conversations, we wrestle with timing questions, including the following:

- **Early Timing:** should I have a conversation now before there is clearly a problem?

- **Early Timing:** what if I speak now but burn a bridge because I didn't fully understand the situation or my approach is wrong?

- **Late Timing:** do I wait until there is clearly a problem and can act with complete certainty? But what if unnecessary harm results by waiting until it's clear there is a problem?

Using early timing, I addressed a potentially difficult situation. I had observed some behavioral issues with a charismatic and well-liked employee. Although others had seen single instances of what I had observed, no one had seen everything I had seen. It was tempting to do nothing and hope the issue resolved itself, particularly because no one was pushing me to deal with the issue. I decided to use early timing, however, and address the issue before it got worse. The employee and I had a difficult but productive discussion, and her behavior improved after our conversation.

In another duel, Musashi used early timing when he suspected his opponent meant to ambush him with a small group. Arriving hours before the duel, Musashi hid in a tree and waited. When his opponent arrived with a small group prepared to kill Musashi, he leapt out of the tree and killed his opponent before escaping.

Business history is full of examples of how timing can be applied to win. Intel during the early 1980s provides an example of using timing in a strategic decision. At the time, Intel's core business was making semiconductor memory chips. After a period of success, Intel found itself struggling to keep up with its Japanese competitors. Gordon Moore (CEO) and Andy Grove (COO) famously asked themselves, "If we were fired, what would the next guys do?" Realizing the next guys would get out of the semiconductor business and go into making microprocessors, they did exactly that. Employing early timing, they acted before it was obvious that Intel could not compete in the semiconductor business. Intel then went on to dominate the microprocessor space.

An example of late timing as a strategy is Tesla. After seeing established auto companies making electric cars, it entered the space with a number of innovations, including an electric-only engine and a luxurious interior. While it remains to be seen how successful Tesla will be, it is a good example of waiting for the competition and then responding.

The concept of timing applies not only to strategic decisions but also to how we deal with our team. And now you will have to excuse me while I go out and check to make sure no one is hiding in the trees outside . . .

One Driveway Equals Ninety-Four Chocolate-Covered Pretzels

There are a great many things I enjoy about living in Chicago, but winter is not one of them. It snowed on Saturday and again on Sunday afternoon. Looking out into the world of white and gray, I saw my neighbor John's driveway was still snow-covered. Feeling restless and looking for some exercise, I went outside and shoveled his driveway. It had been a light snowfall, and because his driveway is short, it only took me a few minutes to take care of it.

I had hardly finished before the doorbell rang. It was John with a box of chocolate-covered pretzels. "Thanks for taking care of the driveway," he said, while shaking my hand. He had just arrived home and was happy he didn't have to shovel. He could have said nothing or texted me. Instead, he made a point of coming over and saying thanks in person and giving me a small gift.

I was genuinely happy about receiving the chocolate-covered pretzels. As I put them in the pantry,

I asked myself, "Why?" It occurred to me that it was because John had said "thank you" while giving me something unexpected. I could easily buy myself some chocolate-covered pretzels, but because he had given them to me in recognition for doing something, the pretzels really meant a lot.

Some people call what John did a "spot bonus," meaning it's done on the spot to recognize good work. As John demonstrated, recognizing good work in the moment is a useful tool. Whether or not you reward someone with a gift card or money is not the real point. We all want to be recognized, and sometimes the best recognition is unexpected, genuine, and in the moment.

When I was kid, we lived in an old house whose exterior peeled and bubbled every summer. Every fall, Dad would have to sand and paint the exterior while my siblings and I helped by holding the ladder or doing other small chores. One of my chores at the end of each day was to clean Dad's paintbrushes so they didn't harden with dried paint. It was not an enjoyable job; everyone had gone off and was doing something else, and I was stuck cleaning the paintbrushes. But Dad always made a point of coming outside to inspect the brushes and to tell me what a great job I had done. He made me believe I had a special talent for cleaning paint brushes and that I was the only one in the house capable of cleaning them to his standards. He was recognizing my work, and it meant everything to me. I began to love cleaning the paintbrushes. It became "my" job.

The key to recognition is that it has to be genuine. One night, Dad came home from a company dinner, and went directly to his workbench and pounded at something with his black-handled Craftsman hammer. I asked Mom what was going on. Speaking quietly, she told me that at the company dinner, Dad had received a key chain with a quarter and nickel encased in Lucite. The quarter and the nickel represented his thirty years of service at the company. He was so angry about the way he was recognized that he broke the thirty cents out from the plastic so he could spend the quarter and the nickel.

From time to time, I think about those thirty cents. The recognition was done so badly and enraged and hurt Dad's feelings in a way that I could literally feel. It's impossible to know what the company was thinking. When recognition is pro forma or done as part of an annual awards program, it can be less meaningful. And, as with Dad, it can also go horribly wrong.

Unexpected, genuine recognition is an extremely powerful tool.

It's used too rarely and represents the opportunity to improve as a leader while making someone's day. And now you will have to excuse me while I see how those chocolate-covered pretzels are doing . . .

Lessons from
the Book of Dad

Fierce eyes, fierce temper, fierce independence. That is
how I think of Dad. Forced to use a walker as he was
dying from cancer, I remember him roaring in rage at
the loss of his mobility.

During part of my childhood, we lived in a small
town at the far edge of the Chicago metro area. We lived
on the outskirts of town not far where the cornfields
started. There was no public transportation in the
town: no buses, no trains, no cabs. We didn't own a car,
and so we walked everywhere: to school, to church,
to the grocery store. There were nine people in my
family, and when we all walked together, it created
an unusual sight. As a result, people in town called
us "the family without a car." It never seemed to
bother Dad that we were outliers who created a mini
parade while walking to church. He was happy living
according to his values and was untroubled about the
views of others.

Years later I was leading a team pursuing a
consulting assignment with a large and lucrative client.
Successfully executing the first assignment would be
critical to winning new business with the client over
time. Winning this particular assignment would be

timely because our core business was shrinking and finding new business was critical to our ongoing survival.

The biggest challenge to winning the assignment was our vision. While we had a clear idea of what should be done for a successful outcome, our thinking was miles away from the client's. Although we understood the client's preferred solution, we didn't believe their solution would succeed. At the same time, our team believed the only way to win the pitch was by proposing the client's preferred solution. Then, having won the business, we would convince the client to do it our way.

I saw things differently. I thought we should be candid and give the client our preferred solution during the initial pitch. If the client didn't like our pitch at the onset, why would they change their mind later? Worse, we didn't believe in the client's solution and weren't prepared to deliver their vision. Our strategy to win the business felt like a bait-and-switch approach. How could we win additional business if we spent our efforts trying to convince them not to do that thing we had been hired to do?

Despite a lot of pressure from the team, I pitched the client on our vision. It was difficult to go against the team and more difficult when we didn't get the assignment. Opposing the team put me in a lonely place. While I had done the right thing, it came at a cost. I found myself criticized and walled off from the team. The team was really tight, and being exiled hurt. While this was painful and I would have preferred to avoid it, I was able to stomach it because I had learned from Dad how to be an outlier, how to be comfortable not fitting in, how to be independent.

On this Father's Day, I can see Dad in my mind's eye, smoking an unfiltered Camel, brushing his comb-over back with his hand, his fierce eyes deep in a book. I learned a lot from Dad. His lesson on embracing discomfort, on being willing to be lonely if you believe you are doing the right thing, is something I find myself coming back to over and over again. Thank you, Dad.

And now you will have to excuse me; I have some paint brushes to clean . . .

Cigar-Butt Leadership

One style of stock market investing is called "value" investing. Benjamin Graham is considered the founder of value investing, and he sometimes called it "cigar-butt" investing. The term "cigar butt" comes from the Depression-era practice of unemployed men scavenging cigar butts from the gutter to smoke the last few puffs. Scavenging from the gutter might be hard to imagine now, when unemployment is 4 percent, but during the Great Depression the unemployment rate reached nearly 25 percent. With so many out of work and competing against each other for jobs, cigars were an unaffordable luxury. For the unemployed craving tobacco, the gutter offered the only solution.

In our roles, we invest in a lot of things, including people. Depending on our business, people create some or all of the value in our business. Like leadership, there is both art and science to investing.

Value investing in the stock market means buying beaten-down stocks in the belief that they are undervalued. Value investors then wait for the market to perceive that the company's stock is too cheap and then sell their investment as the share price of the company rises.

Warren Buffet credits much of his investment success to the lessons he learned from Ben Graham. Buffet, however, points out that he made a number of investment mistakes by buying cigar-butt companies. In many cases, the companies he bought were cheap for a reason: they weren't very good companies and were destined to stay in the gutter.

We can learn from Buffet's pain. While it's tempting to try and wring out the last bit of value from a person or a strategy, some things can't be fixed. Our egos might feel good when we believe we see hidden value, but what if we are wrong and just wasting our efforts?

When an investment is being bought, it means the seller perceives little future growth while the buyer sees strong upside. Similarly, two people can come to vastly different conclusions about the value of an employee. For example, a former colleague named Betty was studying for a test that would allow her to leave her current role and get a much better-paying job. Betty's supervisor assumed that after passing the test she would leave the company, and saw Betty as a short-term employee. The supervisor was, in effect, a seller. In the meantime, I was impressed by Betty and thought she would go on to a very successful career. Seeing her upside, I was a buyer. Believing we should find a way to keep her, I arranged for her to apply for a job in another department. Betty's story had a happy ending: she passed the exam, transferred to the other department, and went on to great success. In this instance, I saw value where her supervisor did not.

On the other hand, I have made the wrong judgments about people, choosing to continue to invest my time and energy in them when I should have been a seller. I recall one instance where despite people repeatedly complaining to me about an employee, I insisted on finding a way to save them, hoping that there would be a change in their behavior. There was no change, and I had to let the person go and admit to myself that I had been a cigar-butt investor who kept trying to find value where little existed.

> It's tempting to think we can see the value that no one else does, whether it's investing in an untested employee or trying to help an underperformer.

To avoid this, we should continually ask ourselves whether we are seeing real value or behaving like cigar-butt investors.

And now you will have to excuse me while I throw away my cigar-butt collection . . .

Don't Go There

Did you ever work for someone and think to yourself, "I will never do that when I am in charge"? Most of us have thought this at some point. Our management style probably reflects not wanting to make the mistakes we saw our bosses make.

Charlie Munger, Warren Buffet's billionaire partner, has made a career out of studying the mistakes of others and trying to succeed by avoiding those mistakes. In his speech called "The Psychology of Human Misjudgment,"[5] Munger talks about his own journey to be less stupid. His speech has been something I return to over and over again as I try to improve as a person and as a leader.

In his opening remarks, Munger touches on the concept of inversion, quoting the mathematician Carl Jacobi: "invert, always invert." Inversion in Munger's view means asking what you don't want to happen and then working out a plan to avoid that happening. As he says jokingly, "Tell me where I am going to die so I don't go there."[6]

---

5   "Charlie Munger: The Psychology of Human Misjudgment (Transcript and Audio)," Farnam Street, https://fs.blog/2013/02/the-psychology-of-human-misjudgement/.
6   Ibid.

Inversion is a fascinating way of approaching the world and one that I am continually trying to understand. I have been thinking about inversion and how it applies to leadership. What wouldn't we want to do as leaders? A lot! Below is a list of the things we can avoid doing:

- **Being on Send:** Simply put, not listening to your team because you are doing all the talking. I vividly remember attending my first Monday morning meeting after starting a new job. Our boss came into the meeting, lectured for an hour, and then the meeting was over. This is what being on "send" looks like.

- **Being a Persecutor:** Being unwilling to accept blame for your mistakes or the team's mistakes and working to make sure others get the blame. If you are going to take the credit, you have to take the blame. If you throw your team under the bus when something goes wrong, you will lose the support of the team.

- **Being a Micromanager:** Telling your team how to do their jobs. There are many, many ways to do something. Usually the person doing the job understands the best way to do their job. If they don't, you have the wrong person, and it's your job to change that person. It's not your job to do their job.

- **Being a Knower:** In our Stagen leadership class, drawing on the work of Carol Dweck, we discussed the difference between being a knower and learner. A knower is closed to learning new things and spends lots of effort making sure it appears they know everything. A learner is on a journey to discover and doesn't let their ego hold them back from learning. If you are a knower, the team can never tell you anything you don't already know. If you are learner, the team is constantly telling you something you don't know, and they understand part of their job is to help you learn.

- **Being an Avoider:** Ben Horowitz, in his book *The Hard Thing About Hard Things*[7], discusses "management debt," where avoiding hard decisions leads to difficult long-term consequences. Examples of things we avoid making hard decisions about include difficult employees, killing underperforming strategies or products, and difficult customers. Better to take the pain now.

As Munger points out, inversion can be a powerful tool. Studying the mistakes of others and making sure we don't make those same mistakes is a useful way to improve and become more effective. Otherwise, you can be sure the people you work with are taking note of your behavior and putting it on their own inversion list. And now you will excuse me; I have to figure out where I don't want to go to dinner tonight . . .

---

7   Ben Horowitz, *The Hard Things About Hard Things: Building a Business When There Are No Easy Answers* (New York: HarperCollins, 2014).

My One-Person Chain Gang

"Did you raise your hand in school today, Jimmy?"

"Uh . . . Mom, you don't get credit in law school for raising your hand."

Mom was the toughest manager I ever met. A child of the Great Depression who grew up in tough circumstances, she was the fiercely demanding CEO of O'Brien, Inc. Her seven children were expected to be number one in their class (a standard I failed to achieve for twenty consecutive years), study hard, and, when not studying, have at least one job. And having two jobs was better than having one. On occasion, she and my dad forged some of my siblings' birth certificates so they could start working as early as age eleven.

Her children were not immune to her demands: six of us have graduate degrees, including two law degrees, an MD, and three MBAs. When teased about being the lone holdout, my sister Kathy points out that she was the only one of us to graduate magna cum laude!

Mom was well ahead of Peter Drucker, who said, "What gets measured, gets managed," and Mom was all about metrics. Every day she asked the same questions designed to give her the answers to her metrics:

- Did you raise your hand in school today?
  As former schoolteacher, Mom knew class
  participation could help raise your grades.

- Did you get any papers back? Mom did not
  believe in being surprised by a report card.
  She took in data throughout the semester.
  Any signs of a poor grade were immediately
  addressed by Mom at your peril.

- Did you get any homework? Doing homework
  took precedence over everything else, and Mom
  wanted to know how much and by when.

- Did the teacher give out any extra credit?
  More than anything, Mom believed in hard work.
  She loved any opportunities for extra credit.
  Me, not so much!

Mom's metrics were good ones for someone
trying to manage seven small children. When she
asked me the same question fifteen years later
when I was in law school, Mom was failing to adjust
to growth. I was older mentally, physically, and,
presumably, emotionally. In other words, what were
once useful metrics were no longer appropriate.

We, too, can be like Mom, using stale metrics no
longer of any real value. For example, I have a friend
named Karen who is a very successful entrepreneur.
Karen dropped out of college to start her own
business and now owns several businesses with over
one hundred employees. Despite her success, she is
still managing her team as if it were a small business.

Karen has failed to adjust to the growth of the business and to the growth of her team. Because no problem is too minor for her, the staff has learned to delegate problems to her. In other cases, they simply passively wait for Karen to identify a problem and its solution. After creating millions of dollars in value in her business, she is now the biggest obstacle to further growth. Despite her acumen and great success, Karen has become a one-person chain gang shackled to a series of small problems that would be better handled by her team.

Why do we join our own chain gang? It is our inability to stay quiet and let our team get on with things. We feel better when we are doing *something or anything.* Murray Stahl, in his vastly underappreciated essay titled "Minutes of the British War Cabinet, September 18, 1940,"[8] perfectly captured this sentiment as it relates to investment management. In his essay, Stahl notes that during the Battle of Britain, the Royal Air Force routinely inspected fighter planes in an effort to keep them free of mechanical problems. To its horror, the RAF found the freshly inspected planes had the highest rate of mechanical errors, even after the inspection. In other words, the very act of trying to prevent mechanical problems led to an increase in mechanical problems. Stahl then brilliantly applies this logic to managing an investment portfolio, saying, "Hence, a diligent,

---

8   Murray Stahl, "Minutes of the British War Cabinet, September 18, 1940: A Non-Mathematical View of the Logical Consequences of Portfolio Turnover," Horizon Kinetics, July 1998, https://horizonkinetics.com/wp-content/uploads/docs/Brittish%20war%20minutes%20%20portfolio%20turnover.pdf.

attentive and active portfolio manager might actually reduce returns. Intelligent inactivity is a rare virtue."[9]

> We can be more effective when we cultivate the ability to leave our team alone except for the critical things that really matter.

And the things that mattered last week or last year or the last decade might not be things that matter today. Anxious to add value, our restlessness and inability to be still creates what my former colleague Stephen Peak called "a rod for your own back."

What would Mom say about all this? She had a tough, sarcastic sense of humor, and she would probably say, "kvetch, kvetch, kvetch," which is Yiddish for "complain, complain, complain." And now you will excuse me; I have some extra credit to do . . .

---

9   Murray Stahl, "Minutes of the British War Cabinet, September 18, 1940," p. 62.

When Things Fall Apart

Murphy's Law . . .

> S*#t Happens
> Things Fall Apart
> Rust Never Sleeps

Most of us have heard of Murphy's Law: "Anything that can go wrong will go wrong." "S*#t happens," "things fall apart," and "rust never sleeps" are all other ways of summing up Murphy's Law. When things go wrong, we are charged with responding. How we respond defines us, both as a leader and as a person.

Last summer my stepson Connor turned up at a sprawling military base to continue his graduate research project. Connor's project involves a long-term forestry study using plots of land at the military base. His summer research required making extensive field measurements with the help of a second graduate student. Unfortunately, the second student had to leave abruptly, and because of the late notice and security clearance requirements, Connor was unable to secure a replacement.

Connor didn't control that Mr. Murphy had shown up and was threatening to wreck his graduate research project. He did control his response, however. Connor had multiple options, including giving up and going home, waiting for his advisor to solve the crisis, or waiting for someone from the military base to solve the problem.

Instead, Connor chose to see the problem as an opportunity. Within hours of learning he had lost half the team for the entire summer, Connor was experimenting with tools and implements that might help him accomplish the research on his own. After a day of trial and error, he devised a way of doing the work without a partner. By using his cobbled together instruments, he was able to accomplish his fieldwork despite Mr. Murphy's appearance.

Things go wrong. Usually at the worst time. It happens to everyone and every company. As Ryan Holiday points out in his book, *The Obstacle Is the Way*, humans have been trying for thousands of years to develop the right mindset when things go wrong. Holiday quotes the Roman Emperor Marcus Aurelius writing in his journal (we now know the journal as the *Meditations*): "The impediment to action advances action. What stands in the way becomes the way."[10] Holiday took this quote and used it as the title of his book *The Obstacle Is the Way*. Mastering this approach to problems is a lifelong journey. It is always easier to complain, whine, or wait for someone else to solve the problem. But when you start looking for examples

---

10 Ryan Holiday, *The Obstacle Is the Way: The Timeless Art of Turning Trials into Triumph* (New York: Portfolio, 2014), p. xiv.

of problems turned into opportunities, they are everywhere. For example:

- **Post–World War II Japan:** Its economy destroyed after WWII, Japan rose from the ashes to become the world's third-largest economy.

- **Apple:** After nearly going bankrupt and being propped up by Microsoft, Apple recovered to currently become one of the largest companies in the US.

- **Ulysses S. Grant:** Facing the annihilation of his army after the first day of the Battle of Shiloh, Grant was visited by General William Tecumseh Sherman at midnight in a driving rainstorm.

   "Well, Grant, we've had the devil's own day, haven't we?" Sherman remarked.

   "Yes," replied Grant. "Lick 'em tomorrow, though."[11]

   Grant attacked early the next morning and drove the Confederate Army from the field.

Sometimes unplanned success creates obstacles. After Neil Young's song "Heart of Gold" went to number one on the Billboard music charts, he found himself being positioned as a middle-of-the-road folksinger. His response was to "head for the ditch." Freed from the constraints of living up to a number one hit, he went on to release albums that were

---

11   Winston Groom, *Shiloh, 1862* (Washington, D.C.: National Geographic Books, 2012), p. 340.

anything but folk, including *Rust Never Sleeps*, an album that established him as the Godfather of Grunge. His success had become his obstacle, and he turned the obstacle into a new way forward that better reflected his artistic aspirations.

We are continually faced with things that don't go to plan. Some things are big problems, like Connor's, and some things are minor. Finding the opportunity within the obstacle is a skill we can all develop. And now you will excuse me while I go wrestle with Mr. Murphy . . .

Doing What
I Was Born For

Marcus Aurelius was a Roman Emperor who kept
a private journal of self-criticism and ways that he
might improve as a person. This journal, discovered
after his death, became known as the *Meditations*.
In the version of the *Meditations* translated by Gregory
Hays, Aurelius writes the following to himself
regarding his reluctance to get out of bed:

> 1. At dawn, when you have trouble getting out
> of bed, tell yourself: "I have to go to work—as
> a human being. What do I have to complain
> of, if I'm going to do what I was born for—the
> things I was brought into the world to do? Or
> is *this* what I was created for? To huddle under
> the blankets and stay warm?"
>
> —But it's nicer in here. . . .
>
> So you were born to feel "nice"? Instead
> of doing things and experiencing them? Don't
> you see the plants, the birds, the ants and
> spiders and bees going about their individual
> tasks, putting the world in order, as best they
> can? And you're not willing to do your job as

a human being? Why aren't you running to do what your nature demands?

—But we have to sleep sometime. . . .

Agreed. But nature set a limit on that—as it did on eating and drinking. And you're over the limit. You've had more than enough of that. But not of working. There you're still below your quota.[12]

Aurelius was emperor for about nineteen years. He spent nearly half his time as emperor away from Rome, fighting wars and putting down rebellions. In *The Inner Citadel*, which is about the *Meditations*, Pierre Hadot says, "What a tormented reign it was! No sooner had Marcus Aurelius ascended the throne than he was suddenly overwhelmed by natural disasters, military and political difficulties, and family cares and mournings, which forced him to engage in a battle every day."[13]

Aurelius could have stayed in Rome and let someone else do the fighting. He could have enjoyed the fruits of being one of the most powerful men in the world. But he stayed true to "do[ing his] job as a human being."

In addition to being willing to do his job, Aurelius was willing to look at his shortcomings. His notes were an effort to look at his behavior and hold himself accountable.

---

12 Marcus Aurelius, *Meditations*, translation and introduction by Gregory Hays (New York: The Modern Library, 2002), p. 53.
13 Pierre Hadot, *The Inner Citadel: The Meditations of Marcus Aurelius*, translated by Michael Chase (Cambridge, MA: Harvard University Press, 1998), p. 3.

This morning when I heard the summer dawn song of the birds at 5:15 a.m., I was tempted to drift back off to sleep, listening sleepily to their song. Instead, I thought about how the birds were up and doing what they were made to do. I thought about Aurelius's exhortation to himself to go to work as a human being. And then my feet were on the floor, going to work.

Most of us don't have the option to choose a life of ease and leisure.

And, like Aurelius, we often face difficult challenges and pain and loss. Aurelius faced wars, earthquakes, plagues, and the death of his wife. He could have easily avoided most of these and chosen a life of ease and leisure. Instead, he chose to do what he was born for.

We can learn from Marcus and demand the best from ourselves, demand we get out of the warm bed to do what we are made for. And now you will have to excuse me while I get out of bed. I've got work to do . . .

Loving Our Fate

Ryan Holiday in The Daily Stoic has written about the stoic concept of *amor fati*.[14] The phrase means going beyond merely accepting what happens to you. It means loving what happens to us even when what happens is difficult. I didn't fully understand the concept until I came across a video[15] by an ultra-runner named Jamil Coury. In the video, he documents his run during a one-hundred-mile race called the Hardrock 100. The Hardrock goes through the San Juan Mountains in Colorado, traveling up and over the Continental Divide. It's a brutally difficult race featuring high altitude, narrow trails, and lots of going up and down steep mountains. During the race, Coury and some other runners find themselves in a pelting hailstorm. High on a mountain with no shelter available to them, their only choice is to keep running. Coury, while wincing in pain, exhibits a simultaneous joy about his fate. It was the video, showing Coury laughing and yelling in pain at the same time, that helped me better understand what amor fati looks like.

---

14 "Amor Fati: The Immense Power of Learning To Love Your Fate."
    Daily Stoic, October 18, 2017. https://dailystoic.com/amor-fati/.
15 "My Fourth Hardrock 100 Mile Run," Run Steep Get High,
    July 18, 2017, YouTube video, 35:55, https://www.youtube.com
    /watch?v=Kvjd9sEVv-k&feature=youtu.be&t=1026.

While I relish challenges, I have always seen them as things to endure, to grit my teeth through. I now see there is a joy in the struggle, of working through the challenge. Our street is subject to flooding during heavy rains, and during one rainstorm, Michelle and I went outside to clear the debris from the sewers, wading through knee-high water. Wearing waterproof boots now sloshing with water, I laughed at how silly I had been in trying to keep my feet from getting wet. When our neighbor John came out a few minutes later wearing sandals, I only laughed at myself all over again.

While these challenges may be stressful and, at times, all consuming, they are not life-shattering.

> The real test, however, is learning to love our fate in the midst of experiencing deep pain or loss.

Last night I had a long conversation with a recovering alcoholic named Adam. He had just passed the one-year anniversary of his sobriety. I was curious about how Adam had endured and overcome the daily temptation to drink. He told me he had done it through a combination of things, including much support from his family, going to AA meetings, and accepting that everything that happened to him was meant to happen. As Adam spoke, his amor fati shone through. He had lost all his material possessions, lost his driver's license, nearly lost his family, and yet he loved that it had happened to him. He loved his fate because only by going through so much suffering had he been able to come out on the other end as a sober person.

Amor fati is something I am struggling with as a leader. We are expected to be problem-solvers who are continually clearing the path to success. It's easy to love our fate when things are going well. Bad things happen, though, and often those bad things land in our lap. For me, it's not yet easy to enjoy these stressful moments, especially when the solutions are unclear or when there are no good solutions.

Adam is a powerful example. Despite having gone to a dark place, he exudes peace and joy. If we can learn to love our fate, we become like Coury and Adam, able to find joy in the storm. And now you will excuse me while I go dry out my boots . . .

Sorcerers and Stupidity

Despite being a conservative Republican who voted for Nixon in 1972, Dad was a curious person, willing to explore many different perspectives. An avid reader, his curiosity introduced me to many counterculture authors, including Carlos Castaneda's books on the teachings of Don Juan. According to Castaneda, Don Juan was a Yaqui Indian sorcerer who could time travel. The books became popular during the 1970s for a variety of reasons, including Castaneda's accounts of ingesting peyote as part of his spiritual journey.

One of Don Juan's teachings was that certain geographic places contained energy fields that could positively or negatively affect humans. Don Juan's teachings were similar to the Chinese concept of feng shui, which seeks to harmonize humans to energy forces present in the universe.

While neither theory has been scientifically proven, it does have an application for us.

Whether we know it or not, we have comfort zones where we operate more effectively than others.

Our comfort zones can come in many different forms, such as emulating a leader we admire or focusing on areas where we have deep knowledge. Charlie Munger and Warren Buffet call this deep knowledge our "circle of competence."

While Charlie Munger is an avid reader, I don't know if he has ever read one of my favorite books, *Novice to Master: An Ongoing Lesson in the Extent of My Own Stupidity*, by Zen master Sōkō Morinaga. I like the book and its title because it resonates with my own journey. "Stupidity," it turns out, is my comfort zone. Although it took me a long time to discover this, my stupidity is a place of strength. I am a generalist and that means everyone knows more about how to do their jobs than I do. As a generalist, I am expert on nothing. When I became confident enough (and it took a long time) to ask dumb questions, I learned a lot more and became more useful to my colleagues.

Stupidity as a circle of competence has led me to funny places. Several years ago, I was invited to attend a dinner where two astronomy professors would be giving a lecture. While I am uninterested in astronomy, the invitation offered the opportunity to see some old colleagues, so I decided to attend. Upon arriving at the dinner, I discovered the other attendees were passionately interested in astronomy and extremely knowledgeable. I felt pretty stupid alongside them but comfortable at the same time—I had landed in my circle of competence!

During their lecture, the professors referred to stars and galaxies as being "bike years" distant from Earth. I assumed this was a scientific term and felt embarrassed I didn't know what a bike year was. After yet another reference to "bike years," I raised my hand and apologized for asking a dumb question and asked what a bike year was. The professors laughed and explained that since it was easier to bike around their campus than to drive, they had developed a private joke of referring to objects as being bike years distant from Earth. A bike year was their estimate about how long it would take to bike to the objects in space from their university.

Upon hearing their explanation, I realized no one else in the room had known what a bike year was, but I was the only one willing to be stupid and ask. This was a great lesson for me about how stupidity is my comfort zone.

Knowing where we are strong and weak is an ongoing challenge. At one level, it means knowing ourselves. At another level, it means knowing the world we are operating in and how things are changing. While Dad was deeply conservative, he was willing to learn more about the things that made him uncomfortable, like a sorcerer who claimed he could time travel. If Dad was still here, I might ask him if he was up for trying some peyote, but I suspect he would say that was beyond his circle of competence. And now you will excuse me; I have to get on my bike and pedal some bike years . . .

Mission First or People Always?

Dad loved reading. As a consequence, in our house the rite of passage was learning to read. When we knew how to read, Dad would take us to the library to get our own library card. And in a house of nine people, having your own anything, including a library card, was a big deal.

Every Saturday morning my six siblings and I would walk to the library with Dad. I would take out as many books as I could carry home. I often walked home reading a book, a habit that led to many near misses with telephone poles and mailboxes.

Since I had more free time than Dad, I would often finish my books before the following Saturday. With nothing else to read, I would move on to reading Dad's books. He read widely and had a fondness for mysteries and detective novels that he passed on to me. As long as he was alive, Dad and I discussed books, and he was always a source of new reading material for me.

Without Dad, I am always on the lookout for book recommendations, and have found Shane Parish (on the website *Farnam Street*), Ryan Holiday, and Patrick O'Shaughnessy to be great sources of recommendations. I have also found podcasts to be a source of new reading material, including a podcast by Jocko Willink. A true one-off, Willink is a former Navy SEAL, the author of two leadership books and the owner of a consulting business. During his unique podcasts, he often reviews and reads from a book on war or a book on strategy. It's not unusual to hear him reading from Sun Tzu or Shakespeare as well as many modern books, often written by ordinary soldiers.

The book that influenced Willink most deeply is *About Face* by David Hackworth and Julie Sherman. Hackworth was a highly decorated Korean and Vietnam War combat veteran who came to believe the Vietnam War could not be won. After speaking out against the war, he left the Army deeply disillusioned and moved to Australia.

Hackworth understood the inherent tension of leadership, where a leader is torn between accomplishing the mission and taking care of his or her team. As he writes in *About Face*,

> [The commanding officer] has incredible power over the lives and deaths not only of a faceless enemy but of his men. Sometimes this power causes a leader to become hardened: he stops seeing his troops as human beings. They become faceless assets to him; he becomes afraid to get close or to feel, instead constructing a concrete barrier in his head to keep out the guilt and the pain of lives lost at his behest. In the process he forgets that though he may give the orders, it is the soldier who makes them happen—or doesn't. He forgets

that if you want 100 percent from a trooper, you have to give 200 percent as a commander. You have to keep the boys well fed and well clothed whenever possible, and well trained always. You have to show respect for them, and you have to remember that every trooper is a priceless asset, not some easily replaced, numbered part to be abused or wasted.[16]

Hackworth's words eloquently illustrate the old military saying "Mission First, People Always." While the tension between carrying out the mission and taking care of our people applies to all leaders, it is most obvious for military leaders.

Some writers have said the saying is backwards and it should be "People First, Mission Always." I think this illustrates the nature of the challenge and its tension: there will be times when the mission dominates, and times when taking care of your people is the top priority. Only you as a leader can decide how to balance them. Hackworth himself embodied this tension; known for being a very tough officer, particularly during training, he did everything possible to care for his troops when they were in the field.

I have stacks of books waiting to be read and a reading list running to hundreds of books. I will have to read for a time, however, before I read anything as good as what Hackworth has written about leadership. And now you will excuse me; I have to go look for my library card . . .

---

16   David H. Hackman, and Julie Sherman, *About Face.* (New York: Simon & Schuster, 1989), p. 269.

Mr. Remainder

I grew up with six siblings. We were all close in age, and our house was noisy, chaotic, and full of bickering and competition.

Some of our competition was for food. While we never went hungry, you never knew if what was available after lunch would still be there at dinner. This became more of an issue when there were seven teenagers living in the house at the same time.

This constant uncertainty about food extended to Dad as well. After coming down for breakfast a few times and finding the milk for his cereal was gone, an angry Dad reacted. Dad had multiple levels of anger, with the zenith being a black rage that was terrifying. His reaction at breakfast was a level or two below black rage: he was mad but rational. In his anger, Dad put into place a new household rule: if you used up something like milk or cereal late at night, you were required to go out that night and replace the item so that others (meaning Dad primarily) would not be disadvantaged the following morning.

While Dad's rule seemed to make perfect sense, it had unintended consequences. Because we didn't own a car and the nearest grocery store was a mile away and the nearest convenience store was a few blocks away, no one wanted to go out late at night and replace the milk or cereal they had just finished. This led to family members leaving just enough so as not to have technically finished it, but not enough to be used the following morning for a meal. Dad bitterly called this result the activity of "Mr. Remainder."

"I can see Mr. Remainder has been here again!" he would roar the next morning as he found there was not enough milk to have cereal for breakfast.

Mr. Remainder was one of my first management lessons. He taught me the difficulty of trying to manage an unruly group who were primarily thinking about themselves. While you might have rules to try and manage them, they would forever find ways to evade the rules to their benefit. Trying to enforce the rules was futile. Any attempt (and Dad made many) to track down Mr. Remainder only led to endless finger-pointing about who had been the last one to drink the milk or eat the cereal.

Bringing a group together and getting them to act as a team has many challenges. To a certain extent, we are all Mr. or Ms. Remainder, wired to look out for ourselves first. Instead, we must set the example by acting selflessly. The Marines have a saying, "officers eat last," which sums up the selfless behavior of an officer in the field making sure his or her troops are fed before he or she eats.

People watch our behavior, and if we act selflessly, then we can ask and expect the same from them.

A great example of selfless leadership was by my former colleague Kevin Loome. Kevin headed up a five-person high-yield bond team in Philadelphia. Kevin and his team had joined from another firm and did everything asked of them to build a successful high-yield franchise. Kevin personally flew around the world, meeting with existing and prospective clients, all while producing very good performance for his clients. However, when our firm announced it would be merging with a competitor who also had a high-yield bond team, the firm also announced that the merged company would only keep one of the teams. Although Kevin prepared and presented a plan on why his team should be retained, it was decided that the firm would keep the competing team instead. As part of this decision, however, Kevin and two people from his team were offered jobs in another city, working with the other team.

At this point it would have been easy for Kevin to take the job and move on, comfortable he had done everything he could for his team. Instead, Kevin turned down the job (as did his colleagues). Using the motto "One Team, One Dream," Kevin and his team went looking for a new employer. Ultimately Kevin and his team found a new company and have gone on to great success at their new firm.

These stories always look great in hindsight. A leader did something, it turned out well, and everyone lived happily ever after. The point here is that Kevin didn't know how things would turn out. He took a lot of personal and professional risk to keep his team intact and employed. It wasn't easy; at times it felt like everyone and everything was against him. He was upset at times and frustrated. Despite all this, Kevin acted selflessly.

Kevin's commitment to his team, even at the expense of losing his job, is a powerful example of how selfless leaders act. I just wish I had known him as a kid so I could have introduced him to Mr. Remainder! And now you will have to excuse me while I go out and buy some milk . . .

Samurai Rules

Over three hundred years ago, the accomplished samurai Miyamoto Musashi wrote a book called *The Book of Five Rings*. It details his insights on strategy, sword duels, and leadership. In it Musashi says anyone wishing to learn his strategy should follow nine rules in order to practice his "Way" (philosophy). These rules have nearly unlimited application in life and leadership. The more I study them, the more I see them everywhere. In this essay I will examine the first three.[17]

Rule 1: Make your thinking free of evil.

This means doing the right thing. Doing the right thing is not always easy, however, especially when it conflicts with your own self-interest.

When I think about this rule, I'm reminded of my former colleague Kevin Loome. During a year featuring a small bonus pool, he voluntarily reduced his bonus so his team could receive larger bonuses at his expense. This is a version of the Marine Corp

---

17   Miyamoto Musashi, *The Five Rings: Miyamoto Musashi's Art of Strategy,* translated by David K. Groff (New York: Chartwell Books, 2012), p. 76.

saying "officers eat last." Kevin did what he felt was the right thing despite it coming at his own expense.

Rule 2: Train diligently in the Way.

Training in the Way means continuous, lifelong learning. We are never done in our journey to become better leaders.

One of my favorite lifelong learners is my friend George Georgiev. I admire the way he approaches the world using the concept of "strong ideas, loosely held." This means he believes in something strongly unless something comes along to challenge his view. If it makes sense to change his mind based on the new information, he does so. George reads constantly and is always seeking new insights. For example, despite being extremely good at math, he has begun teaching himself math again to be sure he fully understands math principles. This is what it is like to train in the Way.

Rule 3: Become familiar with all of the arts.

We can find insights and inspirations anywhere. Musashi studied calligraphy, painting, poetry, and sculpture in the belief that once you know the Way, you see it in all things.

When I think about this rule, I think about my friend Bruce, who invented a coating material used on medical devices. Bruce's invention came after studying racing engines. He has a passion for racing cars, and his interest in the art of racing gave him valuable insights as an inventor. In this world of narrow specialization, seeing the relationships between unrelated things like medical devices and racing engines is much like the duelist Musashi studying calligraphy.

We can learn from Musashi's advice. Doing what is right, continuing to learn, and looking beyond the business world for insight are all things that will help in our journey. And now you will excuse me while I work on my calligraphy . . .

Samurai Rules: Part Two

In my last essay I touched on the first three rules of the Way, as described by the samurai Miyamoto Musashi. These rules—think of what is not evil, train in the Way, and take an interest in all the arts—can show up in unexpected places, like the medical device inventor who was inspired by his passion for racing engines. In this essay I touch on Musashi's fourth, fifth, and sixth rules.[18]

Rule 4: Understand the Ways of all the professions.

As lifelong learners, we benefit from a broad view. Everything you have done will help you with what lies ahead. Lessons learned from colleagues and friends and relatives can add to your knowledge, as does studying the lives of people in other professions.

Marc Andreessen, the founder of Netscape and a venture capitalist, reads biographies of individuals

---

18 Miyamoto Musashi, *The Five Rings: Miyamoto Musashi's Art of Strategy*, translated by David K. Groff (New York: Chartwell Books, 2012), p. 76.

who enjoyed success from the time period 1870 to 1930. For Andreessen, those sixty years represent a disruptive time similar to today. By studying the lives of people who succeeded during an environment like the one we are living through now, Andreessen hopes to learn how to respond to our current challenges. Despite his success and accomplishments, he is committed to continuous learning.

Andreessen offers a powerful example of not only being a lifelong learner but also thoughtfully discerning where lessons might be found. Remaining a student and choosing an area of focus can be useful for all of us.

Rule 5: In all things, discern profit from loss.

We should aspire to see that everything has positives and negatives. For example, being the dominant leader in an industry has an upside and a downside. While being on top has obvious advantages, it can also lead to complacency or make the company vulnerable to industry disruption. Conversely, a small player can be nimble and quick while having to overcome the disadvantages of being unable to set the pace in the industry.

When I spoke with David, the CEO of a small investment firm, we discussed his challenges. David has inherited some problems that make it difficult to grow the business via a merger or an acquisition. This would seem to be a negative, and some CEOs might choose a strategy of repairing the business and leaving M&A for another day. Instead, David is examining how he can create alliances and minority stakes with other companies for their mutual benefit. By using alliances, he hopes to fill in the company's gaps despite its inability to do M&A. David sees the positive and negatives in his current situation and is acting accordingly.

Rule 6: Learn to evaluate everything.

It's easy to miss seeing things clearly. We focus on a small issue and end up missing a larger one. Or we spend a lot of time considering the faults of a colleague while missing our own.

At my Stagen Leadership Academy course we studied the concept of "the story I am telling myself." The story I am telling myself asks us to consider whether we are seeing things accurately. It encourages us to tell others how we are seeing things and ask them how they are seeing the same things. By developing a habit of asking if a different conclusion could be reached from the same facts, we learn to see things we might have otherwise missed.

And now you will have to excuse me; I have some professions to study . . .

Samurai Rules: Part Three

In my last two essays I touched on the first six rules of "the Way," as described by the samurai Miyamoto Musashi. These rules—think of what is not evil, train in the way, take an interest in all the arts, know the way of all professions, know the advantages and disadvantages of everything, and learn to see everything accurately—are the distilled wisdom of a warrior who traveled around Japan during the Middle Ages, testing his fighting skills and seeking to survive during a chaotic period. In this essay I touch on his seventh, eighth, and ninth rules.[19]

Rule 7: Realize and understand that which cannot be seen.

How do we do this? How do we see things that are hidden from view? It begins with having a mindset to look for clues and signals. When we begin looking, the clues and signals are often in plain sight.

---

19 Miyamoto Musashi, *The Five Rings: Miyamoto Musashi's Art of Strategy*, translated by David K. Groff (New York: Chartwell Books, 2012), p. 76.

A favorite phrase of mine is "watch the feet." Watching the feet means sometimes people say one thing and then do something else. By watching the feet, we can understand what is true because the feet (meaning what someone is doing versus what they are saying) tell us. For example, if a leader tells her team it's important to arrive on time for meetings but turns up late herself, the team will watch the leader's feet and understand the leader does not believe being punctual is important.

Rule 8: Notice even the slightest thing.

Many big problems begin as small ones. We should aspire to see how the little issues can become larger ones and seek to fix them before they turn into a crisis.

Years ago, I worked for a division having trouble making its payroll. The payroll problem was so bad that the division found it difficult to timely make 401k fund contributions. Because they represent employees' retirement savings, the government is tough on companies failing to timely make 401k fund contributions. Rather than appeal to our corporate parent for funds to make the 401K contributions and risk the parent company's displeasure, the division treasurer made the contributions only as cash flow permitted. The treasurer therefore violated the 401k regulations and created a much larger problem for himself, the company we worked at, and the parent company. When the late funding was discovered, the company was suddenly faced with a time-consuming and costly cleanup project that also damaged morale when employees learned their 401k contributions had not been made on time. Had the treasurer chosen to be careful in this small matter, much hardship and bad feeling would have been avoided.

Rule 9: Don't do things that serve no purpose.

This endless application for all of us. Mindlessly looking at social media, doing reports that go unread, and holding low-value meetings are all examples of things that might be useless.

At one company, I found myself attending a weekly meeting that was of little value to me. Issues were endlessly debated, while decisions were rarely taken. Inspired by Musashi, I quietly stopped attending the meetings. The result: I was happier, the meetings continued without me, and the world kept turning.

Musashi's rules are more than three hundred years old and represent timeless wisdom. People like Kevin and George and Marc Andreessen are all on the Way. By observing them, we can learn from them as they put into practice Musashi's rules. And now you will excuse me; I have to go decline some meeting invitations . . .

"Florida Has Been Very, Very Good to Me"

It's human to ease up after working hard and enjoy well-deserved success. While attending a conference, I heard a consultant specializing in the turnarounds of failing businesses give a lecture on the mistakes he had seen during his career. "Florida has been very, very good to me," he said. What he was referring to was the tendency of some successful small-business owners living in the north to run their business remotely from Florida each winter. With their business doing so well, it seemed as if they could operate the business from afar while staying warm. But as little problems arose, they either didn't see them or ignored them, allowing complacency to creep in. The consultant's point was that it is during the good times that the seeds of failure are sown.

After the Chicago Bears reached the playoffs for the first time in eight years, their success inspired me to read a book by Rich Cohen called *Monsters: The 1985 Chicago Bears and The Wild Heart of Football*. The book covers the team's only Super Bowl to date. In it, Cohen interviewed Mike Ditka, the Bears coach, and asked him why the Bears, one of the most dominant football teams ever, were unable to repeat as Super Bowl champions. Ditka answered by saying, "Maybe winning is the greatest thing that can happen to a team and also the biggest disaster. It's never the same after you win."[20]

Ditka's answer echoes a Japanese saying: "*Katte kabuto no o wo shimeyo.*" This means, "After victory, tighten the helmet strap." The saying means success brings complacency. After achieving success, you must guard against the natural tendency to ease up. Instead, you should redouble your efforts while expecting tougher challenges ahead.

Complacency is one of the toughest challenges we face. It's everywhere.

In good times, we are tempted to ignore cracks in the foundation of our success. In good times, it's easy to ignore these things because they are small and everything else is going so well. It's only over time, as the business begins struggling, that we can look back and see how our problems began during the good times.

Complacency sneaks into our egos as well. When things are going well, it's easy to credit ourselves for the success when actually many people helped create the results. As people congratulate us and ask us for insights and advice, it's easy to rewrite history and see ourselves as the sole reason for success.

---

20 Rich Cohen, *Monsters: the 1985 Chicago Bears and the Wild Heart of Football* (New York: Farrar, Straus and Giroux, 2013), p. 106.

This played out in a division where I was working. After a long struggle, the team was finally enjoying enormous growth and success. The division's success was the result of dozens of people's hard work as well as some courageous decisions by senior management. As time wore on, however, a halo went up around my head. People began congratulating me for the division's success as if I alone was responsible. At these times, it was difficult to remind myself I had been a modest contributor at best.

What can we do to tighten our helmet straps? We can be honest with ourselves about the source of our success. Did we show up at the right place, at the right time, and get lucky? Or did we make mistakes that a rising market covered up? We can go searching for our Floridas, those things that demonstrate we are letting up and coasting. Lastly, we have to acknowledge Ditka was right: it is never the same after you win, and success means we are never the same again either. Winning is hard, but staying on top is harder.

And now you will have to excuse me while I cancel my winter trip to Florida . . .

Part II

LESSONS LEARNED FROM RUNNING

Late March and
Suddenly
The ice is off the lake
On our long run
We ran on the old Indian trail
Alongside the deep lake
You stopped atop Teddy's Hill
Waiting for me
Looking down at the new blue waters

Endure vs. Embrace

I came late to running, and reluctantly. I had always seen running as painful and something to be avoided. And if it couldn't be avoided, then it could be endured. At the first company I worked at, the president religiously jogged three miles a day. Every July he sponsored a three-mile company race, and everyone in the company was expected to participate in the race or work as a volunteer. In my first year at the company, I signed up to run the race and gave myself a week to prepare. My minimal preparation proved to be a mistake, resulting in a painful run, and I hobbled around the office for a few days after the race.

But the race and the competition that came along with it began to intrigue me. Although three miles seemed a long way to run, the following year I found myself wanting to improve on my time from the prior year. Learning my lesson about starting training too late, I began running during the spring. Later, I joined the company running club so I could stay in running shape all year. I still found running painful and something to be endured, but I enjoyed racing and competing against others.

I kept running longer distances and started running marathons. At the start of one marathon, I saw someone wearing a shirt that said, "Pain is inevitable.

Suffering is optional." I liked the saying, but I didn't really understand it. Only after running about thirty more marathons did I see that suffering was a choice. I went from seeing running as a painful endurance test to seeing it as something to be embraced.

Leadership can be painful.

Things don't go to plan, or we find ourselves unexpectedly criticized despite acting with the best intentions. We can choose to endure these problems and enter "the pain cave," as some long-distance runners call it, or we can embrace the challenge.

I have a friend named Terry who cofounded a start-up business. Busy with many things, he stepped away from the business and turned it over to a cofounder named Ted, who became the CEO. The firm overcame many challenges and, after receiving its first round of venture capital, seemed poised for great success. Ted abruptly announced he was leaving for his dream job, stunning Terry and the team. Terry responded by embracing the challenge. While acknowledging to the team that Ted's departure would make things more difficult, Terry communicated his confidence in them. Seeing that Ted's departure would upset investors, he organized the team to proactively contact investors and reassure them. Finally, he asked the team to consider how hard this decision was for Ted, who had put so much into the business. Rather than gritting his teeth, Terry gracefully embraced the challenge, and instilled a huge level of confidence in the team and the investors by doing so.

Endure vs. Embrace is a useful way to reframe our challenges. Despite the pain, we don't have to grind it out as I did with my first three-mile race. Instead, by embracing our difficulties, we have the opportunity to demonstrate grace under pressure, as Terry did when Ted resigned. And now you will excuse me while I go embrace a five-mile run . . .

Staring at Our Fears

Suddenly and without warning, my brother Peter's heart stopped last November. Despite eating well, exercising regularly, and running a couple marathons a year, his heart quit working, suffering from what is called "ventricular fibrillation" or "v-fib." Peter's wonderful coworkers at Northern Trust performed CPR on him and shocked his heart into restarting with a defibrillator. Ten days later, Peter walked out of the hospital with a pacemaker, a concussion from hitting a filing cabinet when he fell, and three broken ribs and a punctured lung from the CPR he received. He enjoyed a miracle, and we are grateful for the efforts of his coworkers, the paramedics, and the hospital staff that saved him.

During his time in the hospital, we had one of those middle-of-the-night conversations that are painful and searing. Awake and in great pain, Pete found it difficult to sleep, and he kept replaying in his mind what had happened. "I don't understand." he said. "I was doing everything to take care of myself. How could this happen?"

That answer remains a mystery. But sitting with Pete in the dark room amid the muffled noise of a hospital, I wondered not "How did it happen?" but "What would happen from here?" How would Pete respond to this difficult circumstance? Would he be fearful and stop exercising and live life at a cautious shuffle? Or would he give up taking care of himself and be angry at the cards he had been dealt?

The answer soon presented itself. Within a few weeks, despite the pain from his broken ribs, Pete was going for long walks, and in April he ran the Illinois Marathon. Pete is a great inspiration to me because he faced down his fears of what might happen and has gone back to running and living life on his own terms.

> Fear is a big challenge for us. Fear of making bad decisions, fear of being too controlling, fear of being too hands-off, and fear of damaging your career are just a few fears we might be challenged with.

There are dozens of fears beyond these. How do we deal with our fears? I am not sure I have an answer. Some people would say confidence, others might say by learning to detach from the moment and stepping outside yourself. Maybe the fear never quite goes away despite experience and training. Maybe all you can do is remind yourself that it takes action to move through the fear. Pete's coworkers took action by administering CPR, and the security guard took action by shocking his heart with defibrillator paddles. And Pete took action by taking those tentative steps in December in a world now forever changed for him.

Yesterday, Pete and Michelle and I ran eight miles along the Lake Geneva Shore Path on a warm, muggy morning. There was a low fog over the lake, fisherman out in their boats, and a lone swimmer steadily cutting through the still water. It was a beautiful late summer morning, and it felt good to be alive. I know Pete felt that way too. And now you will excuse me while I go face some fears . . .

Local Knowledge

While traveling to Dallas, I found myself trying to squeeze in a long run. As part of training for an ultramarathon, I needed to get in a twenty-mile run. My ideal course would be one where I could run out and back (meaning run ten miles in one direction and then turn around and run ten miles back the same way), have little car and street traffic, and be in a park or trail if possible. Last year I had briefly run along the Trinity River in Dallas, and after using Google Maps and studying the path that runs along the Trinity, I chose to run there. Away from traffic, the path went through wide-open spaces and looked on the map as if it went on for miles and miles.

Setting out on my run, I wound my way through Uptown, past Dealey Plaza where President Kennedy was shot, and got on the trail at the Commerce Street Bridge, next to a corrections center. I had remembered the path as being paved, but the pavement soon gave out and turned into a mixture of gravel and dirt. It had rained heavily, and the path was flooded in places and soft and muddy in others. After a couple of miles, the gravel disappeared into a dirt path. The dirt path was fine for running until it became muddier and muddier. There was standing water on either side of the path, and it was impossible to avoid the mud. Plowing along, my shoes soon became encased with enormous chunks of mud. The mud made my shoes much heavier, and I felt as if I was wearing Frankenstein's running shoes. Periodically I would stop and try to wipe the mud off my shoes, but within a couple hundred yards they would again be encased in giant mud blocks.

I tried to be optimistic, thinking that if I just ran a little further, I would find higher, dryer ground. Eventually, however, I had to admit failure. The path remained muddy, and the run was becoming tedious. Rather than turning back through the mud, I decided to climb a steep embankment where I thought there was a highway. My thinking was that when I reached the highway, look for a new route.

Climbing to the top of the embankment, I found no highway. Instead, I found a level, dry gravel road that exactly paralleled the muddy path I had been running on down below. I had been running at the bottom of a muddy levee while missing out on the dry road at the top.

Standing atop the levee, I had mixed feelings. On the one hand, I felt stupid about my muddy march that could have been so easily avoided. On the other hand, I was happy to have solved my problem and have a dry path to run on. With twelve miles and a couple of hours left, I had plenty of time to think about what I could have done differently. One thing I should have done was to admit my lack of local knowledge. Despite knowing I was unfamiliar with the area, I didn't ask any questions of locals or do any research beyond glancing at Google Maps. I was also too committed to my original plan. If I had gone up the embankment as soon as the path became muddy, I would have arrived at a much better place much sooner.

I also thought I knew what I knew. Believing there was no road at the top of the embankment, I didn't question my belief or bother to confirm it. A quote often attributed to Mark Twain says, "It ain't what you don't know that gets you into trouble. It's what you know for sure that just ain't so."

As I ran along the embankment, I thought about the leadership lessons the run was offering me.

We are at risk of making our biggest mistakes about the things we know for certain.

Having run on the path before, I was certain it was paved. I was so certain that I didn't study the path in detail, only looking enough to see if it ran for a long distance and was away from traffic.

When we are certain, we make decisions without getting input from our team or we override our team's input. Since I was certain, I didn't seek out the local knowledge that was easily available.

When we are certain, we also override or ignore facts that don't fit our view of the world. During the first couple miles of running along the path, I was struck by how deserted the path was. Running next to a large city with a population of 1.3 million, I saw only one person. Why was that? I chose to ignore this red flag, and even when the path became muddy and had no other tracks in it, I pushed on.

Something Michelle and I talk about it is how running teaches us the skill of recalibrating. Runs rarely go as we think they will. Part of our love of running is the joy we find in navigating the twists and turns that a run offers us. Out along the Trinity River, I was slow to recalibrate, and compounded all my earlier mistakes by stubbornly sticking to the plan.

Leadership is all about recalibrating. The world is a messy, complicated place full of complex people (including us). Rarely does something go to plan. It is our job to constantly recalibrate as things change and evolve. Sometimes it's easy to get stuck in a mindset of making the plan work as first conceived while forgetting the plan is there to deliver results.

I would like to say I learned a lot along the Trinity River, but that's not correct. Rather, I relearned some things I thought I already knew. And now you will have to excuse me while I clean the mud off my Frankenstein-like shoes . . .

University of Ultramarathon: Six Business Lessons from Running One Hundred Miles

From the time I was a small boy, I have suffered from an inner restlessness, a need to be outside and moving and looking up at the sky. As an adult, this restlessness slowly ripened into a love of running—first, just three miles a few times a week; then, longer runs; and, eventually, running marathons (26.2 miles). Yet the farther I ran, the farther I wanted to run. I began to dream of running a hundred miles and of running for an entire day and night. I dreamed this dream for a long time until November 2017, when I ran my first one-hundred-mile race. After the race, I realized there were lessons from the run that applied to many things, including leadership.

Have a Plan

It's easier to reach your goals if you have a plan. You can develop your own plan or ask an expert. Asking an expert can be helpful, as it gives you a feel for what is required. For my training, I went online and downloaded a training plan for people doing their first hundred-mile ultramarathon. Much to Michelle's amusement, the plan was for women (thank you, Ultra Ladies™![21]), and it worked very well.

How often do we decide to do something and make it up as we go along? Or develop a plan without getting input from others or looking at the outside market? Have a plan and ask others for feedback. Be a learner.

Assemble Your Team

Sometimes it is better to be lucky than good, and I really got lucky with my team. Ultramarathoners often use a "crew" to help them get through the race, and I had three people in my crew: Michelle, an accomplished runner with over thirty marathons to her credit; Michelle's son Connor, a sub-three-hour marathoner who has hardly scratched the surface of his talent; and our friend Adam Kimble, a professional ultramarathoner and coach. I could not have finished the race without them.

I cannot over emphasize the contributions of the crew. It took me about twenty-five hours to run the race, and the crew only slept a few hours in their cars during my run. They supported me by meeting me at

---

21 Ultra Ladies, https://www.ultraladies.com.

aid stations and making sure I had good nutrition and hydration. Michelle, Connor, and Adam took turns running with me for the last fifty miles, including some very slow miles during the middle of the night.

When it comes to managing teams, I agree with Ray Dalio's approach when he says, "Think of your teams the way that sports managers do: No one person possesses everything required to produce success, yet everyone must excel."[22]

In assembling a team, we sometimes make compromises that we wouldn't make elsewhere. Sometimes people are appointed to the team for political reasons or because they have a loud voice, or it's easier to put them on the team rather than explain why they *aren't* on the team. Yet we always know at a gut level whether we have the right team. Who do you want with you when it's the middle of the night, you have twenty miles left to run, and you are sleep-deprived and cranky? Assembling the right team is within our control and is critical to achieving our goals.

Be Honest with Yourself

I wasn't totally honest with myself about the plan. The Ultra Ladies suggested it would be wise to run a fifty-mile race before running a hundred miles. I chose to ignore their counsel, and this caused me some doubts as to whether I could run a hundred miles. Not running a fifty-mile race also led me to make

---

22 Ray Dalio, *Principles: Life and Work* (New York: Simon & Schuster, 2017), p. 412.

some mistakes in training, including not fully testing my nutrition.

Are you honest with yourself about your plan? What would happen if it cost twice as much and took twice as long? Have you asked others, including the team, for feedback about the plan? It's much easier to have a successful outcome if the team has offered input about the plan and believes they can successfully execute it.

Do the Work

My first challenge was completing each week's mileage. The plan called for a gradually increasing weekly mileage that rose from thirty-five miles in week 1 to seventy-three miles in week 23. This was daunting since I often don't run seventy-three miles in two weeks, much less in one week! As part of this challenge, I needed to avoid overuse injuries. My solution was to focus on not missing runs and being diligent about stretching and foam rolling.

Are you asking what could derail your project? Are you asking how you could avoid these things happening? Do you have a plan B?

Recalibrate As Needed

When things don't go to plan, you can be stubborn and grind forward, or you can recalibrate. During my training I had to recalibrate several times. During my first twenty-five-mile run, I slipped on wet pavement and hurt my knee. Although I tried to continue running, it was too painful, and I had to call Michelle for a ride home. It was tough to quit mid-run, but in a few days I recovered enough to return to running. Quitting in the short term helped me achieve my longer-term goal of completing the training. Other examples of recalibrating included starting a thirty-mile run in the dark to avoid the heat on a ninety-degree day and rescheduling runs to accommodate my schedule.

Are you willing to listen to the market, to the customer, to the competition as you begin executing your plan? The world gives us constant feedback on how our plan is proceeding, but it is not always easy to listen, particularly when our initial thoughts are wrong. Do you have a process for receiving and assessing feedback? Do you actively look for feedback that doesn't match your views or expectations? One of the biggest mistakes we can make is to stubbornly refuse to recalibrate when it's clear our initial thinking was mistaken.

After-Action Review

An after-action review is a reflection used to capture lessons learned after the project is complete. Reflecting on what went well and what didn't go well brought out the following for me:

Went Well: I had a great team and I did all the training to prepare for the run. I finished the run in just under twenty-five hours, which was a great result for my first hundred-miler.

Didn't Go Well: I made mistakes in nutrition. I didn't test different foods during my training and didn't have a plan B if my stomach got upset. When my stomach rebelled at mile thirty-seven, I didn't have other food available, and my crew was forced to scrounge from other runners. And while I tried to apply the Navy SEAL saying of "two is one and one is none" by having plenty of changes of clothing and first aid for blisters, I didn't bring two pairs of gaiters (a piece of gear that goes over your ankle to keep out rocks and dust). When the pair I was wearing broke during the race, it was an unnecessary distraction. I also failed to fully test my headlamp and had to revert to a backup after five hours of use. Without some of these mistakes, particularly around nutrition, I might have achieved the goal of every ultramarathoner: to run one hundred miles in under twenty-four hours.

My completing the after-action review led Michelle and I to agree that I should do another ultra in 2018. (I did run another ultra in 2018 and finished in about twenty-two hours and forty minutes—I was thrilled!)

How often do you do an after-action review? It is just as important to do a review after a success as it is to do one after a failure. Success sometimes occurs randomly or through good fortune, and we should be careful to ask ourselves why we succeeded as much as we failed.

We often face difficult challenges, many of them harder than running one hundred miles. We can overcome these challenges with planning, training, recalibrating, a great team, honesty, and lessons learned from after-action reviews. And now you will excuse me while I go outside and start running; I am feeling restless . . .

Tight Looseness

As a boy, I loved reading the Hardy Boys detective novels, featuring brothers Frank and Joe Hardy and their dad, Fenton. Somewhere in the books it was mentioned that Fenton Hardy was from Boston, and because Dad was from Boston, I asked him if he knew Fenton Hardy. "Of course, I do," he said, and went on to tell me about meeting Fenton Hardy. I was thrilled. Dad knew the father of the Hardy Boys! It was only much later that I discovered the Hardy Boys were fictional characters.

Dad has a talent for connecting with children, whether it was telling me he knew Fenton Hardy or giving the kids in the neighborhood wheelbarrow rides. Dad also understood the need children have for "tight looseness." Children want to be loved and held closely, but they also want their independence. Much of childhood is a tug-of-war between wanting to be taken care of versus wanting to be independent.

I was thinking about independence around mile fifty-five during the Tunnel Hill 100, a hundred-mile race in Vienna, IL. My daughter Colleen was running with me in the cold, dark night as we ran along an abandoned railway that is now a bike trail. The temperature was in the twenties, and some of the energy gels I was planning on eating had begun to freeze into solid blocks. I mentioned this to Colleen while shifting the gels into an interior pocket, where I hoped they would thaw. Colleen suggested I give her the gels to put in her coat pocket, where she had some hand-warmers that emitted a gentle heat. She thought the hand-warmers would quickly thaw the gels.

"That's okay," I said. "I will just put them in my pocket."

I immediately regretted my words. I had asked Colleen and her husband Joe to come to the race and help "crew" me, and she was doing exactly what I needed her to do. Except that I was stubbornly refusing her help. I was acting like a tight-loose child, caught between wanting to be taken care of and wanting to be independent. Colleen was being helpful; she had a better solution, and I was rejecting it because I was uncomfortable having her help me.

"Here," I said. "Put them in your pocket." And we ran on toward the crescent moon hanging in the southeastern sky.

Leadership is complicated. On the one hand, it can feel like our job is to think great thoughts and lead the way forward while everyone else follows us. On the other hand, we want and need the support of the team, just like I needed the crew to help me run a hundred miles at Tunnel Hill.

Collaboration at Tunnel Hill meant I had to give up some independence and let the team help me. It's the same in a leadership role. It won't be your decision, done your way. But by tapping into the knowledge of the people closest to the work, you are likely to realize a better discussion and a better decision.

Tight-loose leadership requires knowing when you need the team's help and knowing when it's okay to go it alone.

Dad's tight looseness was inspiring: after he retired, he joined the Israeli Army because he wanted to see and experience Israel as if he lived there. It took an independent mindset to do this (as well as a lot of convincing of the authorities). Yet Dad could also be perplexing and contradictory: he never had a driver's license during my lifetime, and had to depend on others for rides while living in an area without public transportation.

Most of us are a bit like Dad. Our tight looseness is useful in some areas and not so much in others. It's complicated and hard to get it right—just ask Colleen! And now you will have to excuse me while I go email the Hardy Boys . . .

The Most Persistent Question

Michelle and I are training for a spring marathon. Today, as part of our training regimen, we ran for three hours, running through the streets of nearby towns and sometimes following the train tracks that run in and out of the west side of Chicago. Halfway, we stopped at a Starbucks for water and to use the bathroom. It was a frigid, gray day with temperatures in the low twenties, and the Starbucks was warm and comfortable. Having stopped, it was hard for me to leave and resume our run in the cold. Stalling at our departure, I began reading the bulletin board in the store and saw this quote from Martin Luther King: "Life's most persistent and urgent question is, 'What are you doing for others?'" This question is one of the most difficult challenges leaders must wrestle with. Who are the others we should be doing things for? Is it our team? Is it the shareholders or owners of the business? Is it the customers? Is it the business itself? And what about us? Where do we fit in?

What happens when we set out to do something for the team, but it conflicts with the best interests of ownership? Or what if the best interests of ownership conflict with the long-term health of the business?

What if doing the best thing for the business means eliminating our own job?

What's a leader to do to resolve these conflicts?

Rarely are there easy answers. During my own journey while wrestling with these questions, I have come to a few answers of my own.

I learned to start with everyone else. Putting yourself first is wrong. It's also transparent to everyone else. By putting yourself first, you will undercut your authority and support. When a leader's actions are perceived as being in his or her self-interest alone, the leader will struggle to find support. For example, a leader who lays people off to preserve his or her bonus would find little support for the decision.

Ask, "What is in the common good?"

For example, a friend of mine told me about some underperforming staff in her workplace. These people are unhappy, performing poorly, and negatively impacting the morale of other employees. The company is aware of this and has chosen to demote them, hoping they will quit. Predictably, no one is happy. Not the staff, not the employees in question, and not their supervisors. In this instance, it would be in the common good to let the employees go. Taking half measures has only made things worse.

Understanding what is in the common good can often be unclear. While working at a sleepy firm, I saw many employees were content with the status quo so long as they kept their jobs. When a new growth-hungry CEO named Al took over the firm, many employees began passive-aggressively resisting his efforts. Al found himself in a difficult position. If he placated the employees, they would be happy in the short term but unhappy in the long term if the company failed or had to be sold. Placating the employees also meant acting against the best interests of the shareholders who wanted short-term growth. If Al accommodated the shareholders and fired some staff to reduce expenses, this might cause the loss of customers and profits, and might jeopardize the health of the business for the long term. Al might also lose the support of the remaining staff. But if Al failed to grow the business, would he be able to keep his own job? When considering different components of the common good, it seemed as if every action available to him was both helpful and harmful. In the end, Al embarked on a series of acquisitions that helped grow the business. The acquired companies infused the company with new talent that soon drove the business forward, leading to a significant increase in the share price. The long-term outlook for the business improved, shareholders were pleased, the staff that wanted to be part of a growing firm prospered, and Al went on to a successful tenure at the firm.

Grow some calluses. There will always be someone unhappy with your actions. There will always be someone critical of you.

Part of being a leader involves finding a way to accept that some of the people you work with will disagree with your decisions.

This is why focusing on the common good is the only way to succeed as a leader. In the example above, the CEO endured a lot of criticism. But because he was resolved to act for as much of the common good as possible, he was resolute in pushing forward.

The tug-of-war between your self-interest and the common good is eternal. Considering what to do is always on a case-by-case basis. Years ago, I was part of a division in the process of undergoing layoffs. The senior team was meeting to discuss who would be laid off, including some of the senior team itself. I had a raging stomach flu, but I came into the office that day because I wanted to keep my job. I believed I had more value to add, particularly in helping grow the business. Between bouts of vomiting, I successfully fought to keep my job. On another occasion, however, I voted for a transaction where I knew I would lose my job—a job I loved. In that instance, I knew the transaction was in the best interests of the common good. While some people including myself would be let go, I knew it was the best opportunity to protect as much of my team as possible. I also believed it would create an environment where the people leaving would be well treated.

The dirty little secret about leadership is that asking, "What am I doing for others?" brings you into constant conflict as one group's self-interest conflicts with another's. All we can do is constantly reassess the common good and move forward.

And now you will have to excuse me; I have to run home from this Starbucks . . .

Running Your Own Race

Two weeks ago, my friend and running coach Adam Kimble ran the Western States 100-Mile ultramarathon. The Western States is the granddaddy of ultramarathons; it's quite difficult to qualify for, and while there are lottery entries, it can often take years to secure an entry. Beyond the challenge of simply running one hundred miles, the race is run through mountain trails in Northern California. It is not unusual for runners to encounter snow as well as temperatures over one hundred degrees in some of the canyons on the course.

A few days ahead of the race, I asked Adam about his strategy. There were some fantastic runners entered in the race, and I wondered how he would respond to the talent and race-day adrenaline. Adam's response was, "I'm going to be running based off of splits (meaning his pace per mile) instead of racing the other runners. Racing other runners often ends up badly at this race. I'm planning to work my way through everybody in the second half of the race."

Using his strategy, Adam passed a number of runners during the second half of the race to finish as the twelfth male runner and thirteenth overall. This was a fantastic result for his first Western States and established him as a top-tier runner in the sport.

Adam's plan that was built around running his own race inspired me. For all of us, it's a challenge to find our style and stick with it. There are thousands of books on leadership with titles like *Start with Why*, *Extreme Ownership*, and *Leadership Secrets of Attila the Hun*. They all have found an audience, although Attila the Hun is currently out of favor. With all these books and theories, it's sometimes difficult to know what we should do. Adam's confidence to run his own race is enlightening.

> While there will always be fads and new theories on leadership, the best style is the one that suits you on race day.

In my self-development as a leader I have looked everywhere for inspiration and insight, whether it's from Adam, my karate teacher, or birds in the garden. And while I have learned from all of them, I still have to run my own race, just as you do too. And now you will have to excuse me while I fill out my lottery entry for Western States . . .

Lessons Learned from My Personal Worst

When I was a kid, one of the highlights of summer was the Fourth of July. It was my brother Pat's birthday, there were fireworks, and at the local park there were a series of Fourth of July events, including a forty-yard dash and a pie-eating contest.

One year I entered the forty-yard dash and felt good about my chances: there were only three other kids, and I figured I would get first or second. The gun went off and suddenly I was looking at the backs of my competitors. There I was in fourth place. I was unable to recover any ground on my competitors and finished in fourth place.

This was one of my first lessons that things don't always go to plan. Since then, running has become one of my best teachers about how to respond when things don't go to plan. These lessons have been the most powerful when running marathons. What running marathons has taught me is the art of recalibrating.

My thirtieth marathon, the Boston Marathon, provided me endless opportunities for recalibration. The race conditions were difficult: temperatures in the thirties, howling headwinds, and a drenching rain that went on before, during, and after the race.

My plan for the race was to dress in old outer clothes that I could throw away after the race started, wear an old pair of shoes while making my way to the start line, and then change my shoes and socks just before the race began. I would be running the race with Michelle, a veteran marathoner, and it would be nice to have her steady pace to keep me on track.

Shortly before the race started, I checked the weather radar and guessed it would be raining for at least two hours during the race (I proved to be too optimistic). Since it would be raining for so long, there was no point in changing my shoes and socks before the race. I resigned myself to running with wet feet. Although I shed one of my jackets at the first-mile marker, I wore my long pants, winter hat, a baseball hat, and a poncho for the entire race. And I was happy to have them. Shortly after shedding my jacket at the mile marker, I realized I couldn't keep up with Michelle, and she soon disappeared down the road without me.

Without Michelle to pace me, I had to fashion a plan for the next twenty-five miles. My plan was to start out slowly and avoid being seduced by a course that goes gently downhill for thirteen miles only to climb steadily for the next seven miles, leaving your legs and ego shattered. I hoped that by starting slowly, face the second half of the course with a lot of strength.

Did I mention that things don't always go to plan?

It never stopped raining, and I never felt strong. By mile thirteen, I realized I was going to struggle for the rest of the race and adopted a new plan, which was to simply finish. In order to finish, I began walking one minute each mile and then running the rest of the mile. The last thirteen miles took me a very long time, and my pace grew steadily slower. Finishing in four hours and fifty-one minutes, I ran my slowest road marathon by at least thirty-five minutes. This is called a "PW," a personal worst.

It was apparent to me early in the race that I was on my way to a PW. This was not the plan, and it took me a while to calm my mind down and accept it. Facing up to my PW, I had to recalibrate my goal from a time target to simply finishing and enduring.

We enjoy unlimited opportunities for recalibrating. Revenues are over or under budget, a project is late, someone is performing really well and needs to be promoted, or someone is not performing well and should be written up. The things that don't go to plan define us because they give us the opportunity to continually reshape our people, our projects, and ourselves. We make the most impact by focusing on the things not going to plan and finding within them opportunities to recalibrate.

After running well in the past, it was hard to struggle on Marathon Monday and not meet my pre-race expectations. It was hard during the race to face up to the fact that I was slowly producing my personal worst time. Strangely, after the race I was very much at peace. I had found a way to respond when things weren't going to plan and was better for it. And while I will never win a forty-yard dash, give me enough miles and I will recalibrate and learn and endure. And now you will excuse me while I go back out on the racecourse and look for the jacket I threw away after the first mile . . .

When Less Is More

The Western States Endurance Run is a one-hundred-mile ultramarathon that goes through the Sierra Mountains in California. The run is the brainchild of Gordon Ainsleigh who, while participating in a horse trail ride along the course in 1973, wondered if a human could run the course in twenty-four hours. The next year, in 1974, Ainsleigh ran the course in just under twenty-four hours, and the Western States 100 was born.

In 2016, Jim Walmsley was on pace to set the course record for the Western States 100. He was feeling good, and despite his pre-race strategy to run conservatively, he took off leaving his competitors far behind him. As he said in *Outside* magazine, "I kept on telling myself the race doesn't start until mile sixty-two . . . But I had just never felt so invincible before. Everything was clicking. It was truly magical."[23] Unfortunately for Walmsley, he missed a turn at mile ninety-three, ran two miles off course, and sat down on the edge of a highway, physically and mentally spent. He was eventually found by race organizers and walked the rest of the way, finishing

---

23 Brad Stulberg, "Jim Walmsley's Insane Day at Western States." *Outside*, July 1, 2019. https://www.outsideonline.com/2094661 /jim-walmsleys-insane-day-western-states.

four hours behind the winner. Walmsley's stunning pace and his heart-breaking wrong turn caught the headlines, and he became famous for what runners call "fly 'n' die," meaning he went out too hard and paid the price later in the race.

Michelle tells a similar story about teaching her first group exercise class. She had studied group exercise intensively, received a certification to teach it, and spent days planning the class. Unable to contain herself, she attempted to have the class do everything she had ever learned. Needless to say, the class ended with an exhausted group still looking to get in shape, just not all in one day.

There is a lesson here for us.

Sometimes we attempt to do too much and overwhelm our team with too many thoughts, ideas, and instructions.

Executive coach Marshall Goldsmith writes about the mistake of trying to add too much value, meaning that sometimes people just want you to listen and aren't looking for your views or solutions.

Holding back is particularly hard for leaders. We want to succeed and make progress and have things go well. In that Walmsley moment when "everything is clicking," it's difficult to slow down and maintain a steady pace. It's also hard to let others take the reins, make their own mistakes, and figure out the best way forward. What can be even harder, however, is when others find a way forward that we hadn't considered or one we might have rejected.

Next time you are telling someone else what to do, ask yourself if you are in fly 'n' die mode. Remember, most of the time a little leadership goes a long way. And now you will have to excuse me while I go attend Michelle's group exercise class . . .

PS: There is a happy ending to Jim Walmsley's quest to win the Western States 100. After returning in 2017 and having to drop out due to stomach issues, Walmsley won the race in 2018, breaking the course record and beating the next closest competitor by more than an hour.

Going the Extra Mile (for the Wrong Reasons)

The toughest marathon I have run was the Stinson Beach marathon in Northern California. Starting on the beach in Stinson Beach, it climbs the foothills into Muir Woods, and then pops out onto the coastal headlands above the Pacific. Not only is the course quite hilly for a flatlander from the Midwest like me, it is a "technical" course full of roots and rocks, which become more difficult to avoid as your legs grow tired and weary.

Beyond the physical challenge, the race also required some mental effort to avoid getting lost. Because there are many trails in the area, the marathon course was marked with pink ribbons. When the marathon runners came to a fork in the trail, the runners had to stop and find the trail with a pink ribbon.

At one point, the race followed an out-and-back course, meaning that runners ran to a spot and then turned around and retraced their steps. On a single-track path like the one in Stinson, the faster runners who are now running back begin to meet the slower runners. Running etiquette requires slower runners to step to the side to allow the faster runners to pass by.

Michelle and I believed we were on the out-and-back portion of the course, but we were confused. We weren't seeing runners behind us or in front of us. Could we be winning the race? Maybe. Still, most of the other runners were local runners who were more like mountain goats than athletes, and should have been coming along on their way back and forcing us to step aside. We decided to keep running and look for other runners. After a mile, we still hadn't seen any other runners, and Michelle said perhaps we were lost. Stubbornly, I refused to believe we could be lost and suggested we run another mile. If we were lost, it meant we were going to post a very slow time after running some "bonus" miles. Who gets lost in a marathon and runs more than 26.2 miles?

At the end of the next mile, I accepted that Michelle was correct. We had missed at least one ribbon and had gone off course. We wearily began trudging up the steep hill we had just come down. We retraced our steps for miles and eventually found the marathon course. I finished the race with wobbly legs and an aching ego. Who gets lost in a marathon? Me, as it turns out!

My experience of becoming lost illustrates what can happen to us when we stubbornly stick to our views. We can become so locked in that we miss the data that doesn't fit our version of the world. At Stinson Beach, I refused to accept we were lost, and I ignored that we weren't seeing other runners. Despite knowing we were some of the slowest runners in the race, I kept excluding this fact and all the other facts that would cause me to admit we were lost.

It's tempting to exclude facts that don't fit our view. At one firm where I worked, we sold two investment products, the second of which was much less popular than the first one. Because the second product had enjoyed some initial demand, I believed it would enjoy more demand in the future. After a period of tepid sales, however, I decided to study the product and understand what was holding it back. During my review, I found some facts I had been ignoring. These included that the sales team didn't believe the manager in charge of the product would deliver the consistent performance required by customers and were therefore reluctant to sell it. I also realized that although the product was far less profitable than the other investment product, we paid the same commission for both products. This didn't make sense and meant we should consider cutting the commission, a move sure to keep sales low. These facts made it clear that the second product was unloved, unprofitable, and unlikely to succeed. After facing these facts, we shut down the product.

> If something doesn't make sense to us, it may be that we are excluding facts and missing critical signals.

For me, when I feel absolutely certain about something, this is often a warning flag that I am missing something. I try to counter this by considering the worst-case scenario, the base-case scenario, and the best-case scenario. By using scenarios, I force myself to consider how I might be wrong. Asking "Where might I be wrong?" or "What might I be missing?" is a way to slow down. It's also a way to avoid getting in some extra miles while running a marathon!

And now you will have to excuse me; I may have just missed a pink ribbon . . .

My Own Personal Superpower

I enjoy running and have a strong preference for running outside. Although running inside on a treadmill is always an option, I quickly become bored and impatient when inside. Running outside appeals to me because it offers the chance of seeing something interesting or cool that I would have missed while on a treadmill.

Today while traveling, I ran a route near my hotel as dawn was breaking. While turning around at an intersection, I spotted a golf ball peeking out from some debris under a bush. The golf ball and bush were in a narrow strip of land next to a concrete sluiceway running parallel to a busy four-lane street. On the other side of the sluice way was a strip mall. I paused in my run to consider how the golf ball had come to rest under the bush. Looking around, I saw that up the block and across the street was a golf course. Someone had made a spectacularly poor shot, avoiding tall trees, a low fence, and the cars in a busy intersection to deliver the golf ball to its spot under the bush.

I grew up caddying and carry with me some unconscious instinct to keep an eye out for golf balls. It's just there, and at weird times like this morning, golf balls show up. Having a superpower for spotting golf balls is not particularly useful. It does point out, however, that we all have our little unique superpowers.

I developed this superpower because the worst thing you can do as a caddy is lose your golfer's ball (a close second is losing one of their clubs!). As a caddy you learn to follow the flight of the ball and line the ball up with landmarks like a tree or house, which you use to draw an imaginary line between you and the landmark. Following the imaginary line, you hopefully arrive at the ball and wait for your player to select a club and make their next shot. As you come up to where you think the ball landed, you look intently in the grass, trying not to miss it by lockingin on the area instead of fixating on any single spot.

We all have our little superpowers. If I have a little superpower beyond finding golf balls, it's paying attention to body language. My parents were intensely private and could be hard to read. Intuitively, I learned to read their body language and, over time, found it was something I do without thinking much about. This superpower has helped me as a leader because it allows me to better understand the people and tap into what they are thinking and feeling.

At one company where I worked, the owner's superpower was math. He could do math in his head well beyond most people and certainly beyond nearly everyone else in the company. The problem was he didn't understand his superpower and was always impatient with everyone else's inability to keep up with him. He didn't understand his own unique superpower, and it caused him a lot of frustration while causing everyone else a lot of fear.

We need to recognize our little superpowers and consider how to best apply them. One of the best examples of someone applying their superpowers to great effect was a colleague I worked with at an investment firm. She had three superpowers: a photographic memory, calculator-like math skills, and a deep caring for her team. Well over a hundred people worked for her, and all she ever seemed to do was go around and talk with people. When combined, these three superpowers allowed her to carry in her head the hundreds of investments held across the business, the risks associated with the holdings, and the hopes, fears, and dreams of her team. She understood her superpowers well and employed them to great effect.

> We are well served when we know ourselves and when we know the others around us. We all have superpowers; some of them are useful, some of them are not.

Investing the time to see them in ourselves and others is time well spent. And now you will excuse me; I think I just spotted a golf ball . . .

The Last, Best Day

In the Midwest, we have seasons. While winter and summer are distinct, spring and fall are characterized by long, violent tugs of war. Spring is a bruising battle between winter and summer, with winter often dominating well into April or May. Then suddenly summer arrives, and it seems impossible that winter ever existed. The tug-of-war during fall is less violent, offering languid, warm days and cool nights and occasional cold days whose gray lowering skies warn of winter. Each year, during late fall I begin to watch for what I call the last, best day. The last best day is sunny, seventy degrees or warmer, and comes after some early winter days. I try to lock the last, best day into my memory and return to it during the winter when it seems as if spring and summer will never return.

Last Wednesday might have been the last, best day. The temperature began in the low seventies and then fell during the day as a cold front with rain came through the area. Thursday was much colder, with temperatures only rising into the fifties. The ten-day weather forecast gave no room for optimism, calling for highs in the fifties and possibly the season's first frost. Yes, winter was coming.

I am training for a one-hundred-mile race next month, and my training schedule called for running nine miles on Thursday when it would be twenty-five to thirty degrees colder than Wednesday. I decided to move my run to Wednesday and savor this possible last, best day during my run.

When I got up on Wednesday, however, I felt stiff and creaky and had to drag myself through preparing to run. I got out the door and began running, but after half a block, I quit and walked home. Running felt too hard, I wasn't enjoying it, and I decided to stick to the original schedule of running on Thursday.

All day long, however, I kept thinking I should have run. As the rain moved in and the temperature began falling, I kept up my self-criticism. My self-criticism only grew on Thursday when I failed to get up early in the morning and do my run. "I will run tonight," I said to myself. And then all day the run sat on my mind, something to be squeezed in between meetings, dinner, and bed. I kept thinking about what time I would get home, what time I would start running, and what time I would finish running. But all my thinking wasn't enough. I didn't run in that evening either: a meeting ran late, a train was cancelled, and then there was only time to either run or hang out with Michelle (I chose Michelle, by the way!).

Ironically, I had just read an article in *UltraRunning* magazine titled "Pessimism Is Your Friend" (April 2018). Written by Gary Cantrell (better known as Lazarus Lake, the eccentric and sadistic race director of the Barkley Marathons), he recounts awakening to a cold, rainy morning when he was scheduled to go for a run. It seemed like a good day to sleep in and run the next day when conditions might be better. Cantrell, however, asked himself, "What if tomorrow is worse?" He then went out and did his run. As he eloquently puts it, "It is never easy today . . . the way you get things accomplished in ultrarunning is by persevering through unpleasantness now, not by eagerly anticipating that it will be easier tomorrow."[24]

Not only was I mad at myself for putting off a run on the last, best day, but I was mad that I compounded the issue by not running the following morning. I had twice failed to follow Cantrell's counsel about "persevering through unpleasantness now."

Over the last few days, I have reflected a lot about missing my nine-mile run and missing the opportunity to enjoy the last, best day, and about all my self-criticism. I am trying to learn a lesson from it that boils down to "Do it . . . now." When I find myself thinking about putting something off, I try to shift to reminding myself "Do it . . . now."

This is an unlimited lesson that applies to many things, including leadership. We have endless opportunities to put things off. I have put off hard conversations, and put off hard decisions on people and on strategy and tactics. I can't think of an instance where putting these things off worked out well. And in the meantime, my deferred actions continued to poke away at me, just like the nine-mile run that I put off and continued to worry about.

What's the good news here? The good news is you will always know when you are putting something off,

---

24 Gary Cantrell, "Pessimism Is Your Friend." *UltraRunning*, April 2018.

and you will always have the opportunity to "do it . . . now." As Cantrell says, "It is never easy today. And thinking things will be better tomorrow is not helpful."

We are tasked with doing the hard things. And that means doing them now.

And now you will excuse me while I get in this week's nine-mile run . . .

Part III

FINDING INSPIRATION IN NATURE

We stalked the owl
Passing silent summer homes
And their tangled property disputes
Untroubled
The owl flew on

What Am I Missing?

While working in the garden, I heard a robin give out a single alarm call. "Uh-oh," I thought. "I wonder if there is a predator nearby?" I had just looked up when a sharp-shinned hawk glided over my head. "Oh yeah!" I thought. "There sure is!"

I enjoy bird watching. While some people keep what is called a "life list" of the birds they have seen during their lifetime, I simply enjoy observing the birds. I keep bird feeders and birdbaths in the garden, and watching the birds is a source of great pleasure.

I have learned a lot from watching the birds.

One thing the birds have taught me is asking myself what I don't see.

For example, some birds begin their fall migration well before summer is over. During late August, I begin to regretfully ask myself what birds are missing from the landscape. Over the course of a few days, I might learn that the swallows have departed. They leave earlier than many of the other birds, and it's always a bittersweet moment when I realize the swallows are no longer darting about the sky.

Last summer I caught the change of the swallows on the day after they left. One day they were all around, zooming after insects, and the next day the sky was suddenly empty. It took me a minute to work out that the swallows had gone and a couple of days to fully accept it. "Too soon, too soon," I thought.

Beyond helping me see the shift in the seasons, birds are great teachers about immediate changes. When a predator appears, birds engage in a behavior called "mobbing." Unable to take on a predator by themselves, a group of birds will dart at the predator, making loud alarm calls. By mobbing, they eliminate the element of surprise for the predator, forcing the predator to find another place to hunt. By paying attention to birds when they are mobbing, I have seen owls, foxes, coyotes, and hawks, often in places where I would have missed seeing them.

The behavior of the birds has a seasonal rhythm. During spring, they are looking for mates, mating, nesting, and raising broods. All these things influence their behaviors: for example, the deep blue indigo buntings I saw for the last few weeks have disappeared, presumably because they have mated and are away in the woods. They will turn up again in late summer, preparing to migrate.

There are analogies here for leaders. Asking what you aren't seeing or what is missing is a way to consider whether you are seeing the entire picture. For example, is someone on the team quieter than usual? More outspoken?

While sudden changes are easy to pay attention to, what do they signal? Without understanding the mobbing behavior, the sound of the birds is just a bit of noise in the background. By asking myself if the noise is mobbing, I sometimes see things I was missing (and sometimes, despite the mobbing, I can't see what the fuss is about). Another way to think about this is to look for the mismatch. Asking yourself what you were expecting to see versus what you are observing is helpful for seeing the world accurately.

While speaking with a former colleague, we discussed his current company. He mentioned the company valued the appearance of being busy; everyone spoke about how busy they were, and most people ate lunch at their desk. I wondered what the people running the firm thought about their look-busy culture. Did they want a look-busy culture or to grow the company culture?

We can train ourselves to be deep observers. Knowing what "normal" looks like helps us notice when even small things change. Seeing the small changes can give us insights about larger issues. When we can see large issues while they are still small, we have the opportunity to respond proactively. By moving smoothly from one issue to the next, spotting and cutting off issues before they ripen into crises, we become calm and effective.

If the leaders at my former colleague's company were attuned to the small things, they might have seen they had a "face-time" culture, which emphasized putting in face time over results. Observant leaders might instead encourage a culture focusing on results and permitting less time in the office so long as results are achieved. Imagine an outcome where people worked less and accomplished more!

Tomorrow morning, while listening to the summer dawn song of the house wren, I will remind myself to keep learning what I can from the birds: their lessons are timeless. And now you will have to excuse me; I hear a robin calling . . .

Not a Hero,
Not a Zero

In the Midwest, we enjoy the company of American robins for spring, summer, and fall. Robins are early-spring arrivals; sometimes arriving in late February, they signal winter is coming to a close, and their appearance always cheers me. "The robins are here!" I say to myself. "Winter is ending . . ." There is a period of time during spring and summer when the dawn song of the robin dominates the morning. Every morning I revel in hearing the robins because it means winter has gone. During summer, robins sing a lovely and mysterious song at deepest twilight. As the sun fades, the robins began calling out, and their evening song is one of the great joys in my life.

The other night was one of those glorious early-spring evenings when it was warm enough to have the windows open. I was working at my desk when a robin began its evening song. The song was evocative and mysterious and overwhelmed me in the same way as a beautiful piece of music. There was something about hearing the robin's song through an open window after a long winter that was haunting and wonderful. We had come through the winter and could enjoy the warm air and the promise of spring.

I have noticed that I soon become accustomed to these lovely songs. Rich and powerful as they may be, after a week or two, they begin to fade into the background. This always bothers me—how can I take for granted these beautiful songs that can affect me so deeply?

There is a lesson here for us.

Sometimes we take for granted the people on the team who are solid performers, the ones who do their jobs reliably and without a lot of drama. They are neither heroes nor zeros; they simply show up and get their work done.

Our ongoing challenge is to continue noticing these people, to take an interest in them, and to make them feel valued. This takes deliberate work and can feel unfulfilling because we aren't problem-solving or addressing the latest crisis. It's these people, however, who make the trains run on time and are sometimes only noticed in their absence—like the robins when they disappear in the fall.

I saw this happen with dramatic effect while working on acquiring a company. The company I worked for had bid to buy the small subsidiary of a large insurance company. After submitting our bid, we were instructed to come to the insurance company's headquarters in California for an interview with the CEO and CFO of the parent company. My boss and I met them in a windowless boardroom and answered their questions. At the end of the session, they told us we had passed their test. Subject to completing our due diligence and agreeing on a final purchase price, it was our business to acquire. My boss and I were excited. We had won the bidding process, and it felt as if we were on our way to becoming a bigger and more successful business.

The CEO suggested we have lunch together and meet Pete, the CEO of the subsidiary business, after lunch. We ordered deli sandwiches, which arrived in brown paper bags, and made small talk with the CEO and CFO. At the end of our lunch, Pete was ushered into the boardroom.

It quickly became apparent that Pete was hearing for the first time the insurance company's plan to sell his business. Predictably, he had a bad reaction. Pete felt the business was being sold just as it was about to enjoy some significant growth. As he spoke, it also became clear he was losing out on a large payday since he and his senior team had financial incentives tied to the growth of the business. By selling the business now, Pete and his team would not enjoy the financial rewards they were close to achieving. The insurance company CEO was unmoved by Pete's remarks and pushed the conversation on to working through the due diligence process and the timing of the closing.

During our due diligence, Pete stalled and shuffled while doing his best to appear cooperative. Our requests for information took a long time to be fulfilled, and the information we did receive was often incomplete. In the meantime, a key employee of the to-be-acquired firm resigned, the potential sale became public, and some key clients put the business on "watch," meaning they were considering terminating their contracts with the company. In the end, we chose to walk away from the acquisition, partially because the turbulence at the firm made it difficult to confidently predict their future revenues and growth.

After the uncertainty of the on-again, off-again sale caused more employees to leave, some key clients terminated their business when the employees left, and the insurance company was forced to wind the business down. What had been a profitable business was so damaged that the only option was to shut it down. It was a bad outcome for everyone, and it only occurred because the insurance company took for granted the people working in the business.

It's easy to focus on the latest and loudest crisis while ignoring those people who are quietly doing great work. When we take some time to appreciate those on the team singing their beautiful songs, we are both better for it. This morning I was awakened at five a.m. by the sounds of the robins singing. I was sleepy and wanted to go back to sleep, but for a minute or two I concentrated on their lovely dawn song. I drifted off to sleep, promising myself to not go numb to the robins this year. And now you will excuse me; I think I left the window open in my office . . .

Go Slow and Make Things

Winter in the Midwest is long and lingers on deep into April. Summer and winter pull spring back and forth in a tug-of-war that often lasts until late May. This year, the last snow fell in mid-April and stayed on the ground for a week, melting too slowly. This seasonal tug-of-war creates a growing season that begins with the last spring freeze around May 15 and ends with the first killing frost around Halloween. As a gardener, this allows me five and a half months to plant and tend my garden. Every day counts in the spring, and I am always excited to begin working in the garden.

Today, riding the crest of lovely spring weather forecasted to continue through mid-May, I was happily working in the garden, pulling at weeds and beginning to plant flowers.

Part of my garden has a southern exposure but suffers from stony soil. This afternoon I was planting state fair zinnias in this challenging location. The state fairs do well in most locations, prospering in full sun and delivering giant, colorful blooms that make great cut flowers while attracting birds and bees and butterflies. As I planted each state fair, I dug a hole in the tough soil, amending it with good, black dirt and then popping the plant into the hole. To secure the plant and keep it upright, I mounded a little bit of dirt around the stem of each plant.

While doing this, I thought about how leadership is like gardening. A gardener tends to her plants, while a leader tends to her people. When a gardener amends the soil by adding good things to it so the plant will prosper, this is the same thing as training an employee for a new role. Or you could think of it as onboarding the plant.

Over time, the gardener begins to understand how plants react when transplanted into the ground. Purple coneflower, for example, droops for the first week after it has been transplanted and needs daily watering. So too would an employee who hasn't been properly onboarded: their performance is suboptimal and features unnecessary mistakes.

A gardener has the most success when exhibiting patience. I find it hard to take the time to amend the soil while planting hundreds of flowers. It would go much more quickly if I could simply pop the plants into the soil. Painful experience has taught me, however, that I will spend the summer regretting my impatience while looking at a patchy garden. Similarly, hiring in haste can lead to many knock-on regrets.

Facebook once had a mission statement that said, "Move fast and break things." With approximately 25 percent of the world as their market share, they have been remarkably successful. It seems to me, however, that leaders should go slow and make things. Leaders should make great cultures, great environments, and great people. This takes time. There will be good growing seasons and bad ones. Mistakes will be made; some will turn out well and some not so well.

Tomorrow I will buy more plants and work in the side garden along the house. There are roses there that seemingly did not survive the winter, and I have to decide whether to pull them out and begin again. There are also plants in the side yard that are growing very quickly. My rule of thumb is that when something grows more quickly than all the surrounding plants, it's probably a weed. I will be patient and let them grow a bit more until I can tell for sure. Despite my desire to get to "done," tomorrow I will be patient, go slowly, and keep amending and planting.

> Leaders, like gardeners, should aspire to having a plan, having patience, and having the courage to recalibrate when things go away from the plan.

Leaders, like gardeners, are forever learning and forever humbled by the challenges they face. And now, you will excuse me while I figure out where I am going to plant the rest of the zinnias . . .

Getting Growth Just Right

After an unusually cold spring, we in Chicago experienced a warmer-than-normal May. The warmer weather permitted me to begin gardening sooner than usual, and my garden is already quite far along. In other words, I am ahead of budget.

Today, while looking at my garden and seeing how the flowers were getting on, I was reminded of my mistake last year. I had been a "stuffer" who planted too many plants too closely together. In particular, I planted too many cosmos together.

By planting the cosmos too closely together, I initially enjoyed a great burst of massed color and was pleased with the results during June. As the summer went on, however, the cosmos became mildewed and, despite my efforts, began dying, and eventually I had to pull them all out. By planting them too closely, the early wonderful massed colors gave way to gaping holes, and the garden was never quite right for the remainder of the year.

Today, while looking at the garden and this year's cosmos, I thought about how we face the same challenge when giving people the right amount of room. Just like a cosmos needs less room than a sunflower, too much or too little room depends on the person.

> If you insulate someone from failing, she may not fail but she is also unlikely to grow. Similarly, giving her too much autonomy without proper training can set her up for failure.

Sometimes a helpful way forward is to give people opportunities that are low risk while presenting strong opportunities for learning and growth. For example, in one instance I invited a talented staff member to begin attending board meetings. Although there was no business reason for her to be there, I explained to her it would be useful in her development. (I did, however, ask the board's permission for her to attend the meetings). Eventually, when she grew into a larger role and began presenting to the board, she was prepared for the board environment and its dynamics.

This year, I am keeping an eye on the cosmos and am prepared to transplant them if they begin growing too closely to each other. Every week brings a new challenge to the garden, and the joy is in the effort to get it right. And now you will excuse me; there is a drift of daisies starting to get out of control . . .

Indigos and Intuition

I heard an indigo bunting today while running nine miles through the nature preserve near my house. Indigos are impossibly blue and one of the most beautiful birds we see during a Midwestern summer. Indigo buntings are a bit secretive; they keep to the treetops unless they are feeding in the morning or evening. Over time, I have learned to recognize their song, and now I "see" them using my ears. Avid bird watchers are adept at recognizing bird songs and can hear an entire world most of us are unaware of. Over time, the birders develop a knowledge bordering on intuition, which allows them to recognize bird songs.

Hearing the indigo bunting reminded me of my classmate Mike in my Stagen Leadership Academy class. Mike has done many things in his career, including running a rural hospital that received the prestigious Malcolm Baldrige Quality Award for performance excellence. Mike was a board member for the hospital when he was asked to serve as the interim CEO. At that point the hospital was losing money and had low employee engagement scores. It had such a poor reputation, local residents chose to visit less conveniently located hospitals. Mike ultimately became the permanent CEO and led massive changes at the hospital. Curious about how all this occurred, I asked Mike what he did to lead the hospital's extraordinary turnaround. Mike cited three things:

1. Undertaking customer service reforms. These reforms were created after a family whose child died at the hospital received indifferent and unsympathetic treatment by hospital staff.

2. Addressing underperforming staff after initially waiting too long to do so. Despite his intuition that he needed to address some of the staff, Mike put it off and came to regret it.

3. Recreating organizational values from the bottom after Mike's top-down imposed values utterly failed.

Mike's discussion about waiting too long struck a chord with me. I, too, have put off dealing with difficult employees. While I intuitively sensed there were problems, I either ignored them or tried rescuing the underperformers. Looking back, better outcomes would have been achieved by listening to my intuition and being willing to make hard decisions.

We intuitively know things. It's acting on our intuition that can be the problem.

Sometimes we want more data or we hope time will correct the problem. There comes a point, however, when we need to listen to the little voice in our head.

In thinking about Mike's insights during my run, it struck me that the three things he cited as leading to the turnaround were born out of pain. This is worth reflecting on. While never pleasant, it's often the painful experiences we go through that change our organizations and us. These painful experiences develop our intuition which helps us in the future. The next time I hear an indigo bunting, I will remind myself that these beautiful birds carry a reminder of how our learning builds up and creates our intuition. And now you will have to excuse me; I think I hear a rufous-sided towhee . . .

What's Your Weediness?

While working in the garden this week, I became intrigued with a weed. I don't know its name, but it's everywhere. I can easily find it because it is growing faster than the other plants, including the perennials. Its growth is so far advanced that if I don't remove it this week, it will be crowding out the other plants by next week.

The weed's ability to grow faster than the surrounding plants is its strength, its "weediness," if you will. The weed's weediness led me to think about other examples of strengths and how they show up. The northern cardinal is native to the Midwest, where I live. A bright red bird, it is easily spotted, particularly over winter when the trees are bare. The cardinal receives its red color from eating the fruit of the dogwood, which produces bright red fruit. Because a bird is most vulnerable to predators while eating, the cardinal has evolved to eat at sunrise and sunset, when its bright red color is harder to see. Cardinals like eating sunflower seeds, and I keep a bird feeder full of sunflower seeds for the cardinals. I can track the passage of the seasons by watching for the last cardinal at the bird feeder. In late December, the last cardinal arrives at the feeder near 4:30 p.m., a dark shape in the dying light. By summer solstice, the last cardinal arrives close to nine p.m. By feeding in the half-light, the cardinal is able to avoid many predators despite its bright color.

How does weediness show up for us? I have had some great bosses, each with their own weediness. One had the ability to see the macro of the situation, and could logically work out how one decision would lead to a whole series of knock-on events. Another boss had a steely resolve—in this case, to grow the business. He simply persisted in his resolve to push the business forward despite significant opposition from many people within the firm. Yet another boss had a powerful ability to listen. Staff would present to him, and he would simply sit quietly, waiting for more. Often, the silence made them uncomfortable, and they would pick up the conversation again, saying more than they had intended.

We all have our own weediness. We must understand our strengths and the offsetting weaknesses they bring. For example, my boss, the great listener, was widely viewed as cold and remote. Saying little, he was an enigma to the staff, and people approached him cautiously.

> Sometimes our strengths come so easily we can't understand why they don't come as easily to everyone else.

For example, I have seen a CEO with an extraordinary mind for math and figures. Sitting in a conference room, he could do near-instant calculations about the return of a prospective investment. At the same time, he found it extremely frustrating that everyone around him couldn't keep up. A tough and seasoned entrepreneur, he didn't understand his weediness.

If you begin to understand your own weediness, you can also see it in others. When a leader can accurately see the strengths of his or her team, he can position the team appropriately. As seasons and circumstances change, as our people grow and we grow, we must constantly reexamine the team and ourselves while seeking to optimize for the best result.

And now you will excuse me; it's almost dark, and I have to go look for the cardinals . . .

Part IV

PERSONAL REFLECTIONS

From White Belt to Black Belt to White Belt Again

I came across my Shotokan karate white belt in a drawer. I have been keeping it as a reminder of learning, of failing repeatedly, and of persistent effort. It's a reminder of what the journey is like from white belt to black belt.

In the beginning of martial arts, there were only white belts. Students who trained hard eventually had their white belts turn black from repeated training. The black belt thus acquired a special status, symbolizing hard work and skill. Today, there are many colored belts on the road to black belt.

I used to have a black belt, and it meant a lot. I trained a long time to get it, and my teacher, Sensei Ortega, probably awarded less than one hundred black belts during his life-long career as a karate teacher. I first trained in karate with my daughter Colleen and then later with my daughters Christine and Claire. It was a great thing to do with my daughters, especially as Colleen progressed and became Sensei's prized pupil.

When Sensei died, I put my black belt in his coffin. Sensei used to tell us about how the real level of achievement in martial arts was to have a black belt that had turned white from continuing to train after receiving your black belt (and he had several black belts that had turned white).

Compared to Colleen, I was a mediocre student. Colleen could learn the movements nearly instantly, and I could not. It required endless repetition for me to learn the things Colleen could learn in a single class. I remember being in a small hotel in Iowa and practicing my karate form, trying to figure out how to do the movements in the small room.

As I kept working to improve my karate, I even put a makiwara in my backyard. The makiwara is a padded punching board attached to the wall or to a two-by-four in the ground. Mine was attached to a two-by-four sunk into some concrete. For months I would go out in the yard every day and punch the board one hundred times with each hand. My knuckles became so swollen and scabbed that someone asked me during a meeting if I was in a fight club.

One day Sensei was driving by my house and discovered me in the yard, punching the makiwara. His opinion of me changed after that. I was doing what he called "chasing it." I was still a mediocre student, but I was grinding and working to get better, and he respected that.

Sensei was an amazing teacher. He met each student where they were at and adjusted his style and demands to their level. But when the student began to progress, he would push hard to bring them to another level they didn't know they had. After I got my yellow belt (first belt above white belt), I was proud and cocky. During the very next class, Sensei had me repeat everything I had done to get my yellow belt. And he ripped my technique apart, criticizing everything I did. I went home in a funk. What had happened?

It took me a long time to understand: having arrived at the next belt level, his expectations for me had grown, and what was okay for a white belt wasn't acceptable for a yellow belt level. It was deeply humbling to advance to each level and then find more was expected of me.

Sensei told me when he first began teaching that he held each student to his own very high personal standards (at one point he lived in the dojo and did nothing but train and teach). If a student wasn't training as hard as Sensei himself would train, he would literally pick them up and throw them out the dojo door, shouting, "Come back when you are ready to train hard!"

"I couldn't understand why I kept losing students," he said about his early teaching career. Sensei learned over time to adjust his style to the student and demand from the student everything he thought they were capable of, not what he was capable of.

There are some powerful lessons here for us. One, we are all on a journey.

We are on a journey, and our staff are on their own journeys.

We should respect where our people are at; not everyone is going to be at the same level or at our level. Two, growth is painful and difficult and does not come easily or at once (except for the people like Colleen!). We should be patient and demanding in equal measure, assessing each person independently. Three, you are not they. So often we expect everyone else to be like us, to have the same values or the same drive or the same world views. When we do that, we become like Sensei throwing his students out of the dojo.

For me, the best part of training karate was the journey. I enjoyed traveling the path of endless learning and endless challenge. Often it was scary and hard. But it was the path to growth and getting better. It's the same for us. We continue to put in our work while traveling from white belt to black belt and white belt again. And now you will have to excuse me while I go punch the makiwara board a few times . . .

The Dawn Patrol

When I was fourteen, Dad asked me when I was going to get a job. After some weak protests about how I needed to be sixteen to find a job, I found myself caddying at a local country club where the age requirement was twelve.

The caddy culture was raw and rough. There was lots of foul language, daily card games for money, pot smoking, and mean-spirited pranks. Like any other job, there was a hierarchy. New caddies were at the bottom and known as "shit caddies" because they didn't know shit.

Shit caddies were given the worst players and the worst tippers. The process was designed to weed out the kids who didn't want to pay their dues. Those who stuck it out gradually became better caddies and eventually began receiving better golfers and tippers.

Part of the progression as a shit caddy was caddying for a group called the "dawn patrol." The dawn patrol were three golfers who were such poor players that they had to start at dawn, ahead of the other golfers. Each member of the dawn patrol had very different approaches to the game: one was mainly focused on retrieving golf balls from ponds and had a giant bag full of old balls; one was a notorious cheater; and the last one was only concerned about how fast each round could be completed.

For a year or two, the dawn patrol were my regular clients. I showed up early, the caddy master gave me the assignment, and off we went, squinting into the sun on the first tee. They were terrible players, and I wasn't a great caddy; we deserved each other. In time, I moved up from caddying for the dawn patrol, was given better golfers, and continued to learn what made a good caddy.

I learned a lot from the dawn patrol. One lesson was about how the people who work for you study you and know you better than you know yourself. As a shit caddy, I knew and could imitate the unique swings of the dawn patrol, I knew the various ways they cheated, and I knew on what holes they would want to stop and troll ponds for lost balls.

Another lesson I learned was that we all start out as shit caddies. We don't know what we are doing in our first role as a leader. Sometimes we get a little bit of training, and sometimes we have to make it up as we go. You do your best and keep learning.

The biggest lesson I learned was from my desire to move up the caddy ladder. I began watching the best caddies and trying to learn from them. They were good. They could read a green, never lost a ball, and had all sorts of arcane knowledge like where to aim in order to make a good shot to a blind green.

We can profit from watching others that are good at their jobs. I remember how hard some of the good caddies hustled when their foursome got to the green. They would rake traps, put away clubs while handing out putters, hold the flag while people putted, and wash dirty golf balls. They also paid attention to how each golfer was playing. They were not only lugging around golf bags and doing their jobs as caddies, but they were putting themselves in the shoes of the golfers and thinking like them. This idea of empathy for the people you were working with was a big insight for me. I started to understand that doing a good job not only meant doing "my job" but also included understanding the people around me and how they were performing in their roles.

The good caddies also sometimes offered lessons on what not to do. Used to working for the best golfers and best tippers, some of them became arrogant. They showed up late, took slow days off, or pouted when they didn't get to caddy for "their guys." The caddy master was keenly sensitive to the caddies' egos. When he felt a caddy was becoming arrogant, he would deliberately give the caddy some poor tippers for a few days. He would bluntly tell them they were getting a big head and that's why they were being punished. In other words, he was giving them a performance review.

I learned from this that you can't stop when you reach the top; the challenges continue.

> If you want to be good, you have to keep working to get better, you have to show up, and you have to do the menial jobs as well as the fun ones.

As better leaders, we have to own this or risk having to start working for the dawn patrol again. And now you will excuse while I go investigate a pond that might have some golf balls in it . . .

Lazy and Cutthroat

While shopping in a grocery store, I saw a handwritten note on the wall. It was near the entrance to the store's back room and written on an 8.5 × 11 piece of paper. Curious, I walked over and looked at it. In scrawling letters, it said, "Effective Immediately—NO OVERTIME without (the owner's) permission." The biggest letters on the note were "NO." The note was an insight into the company's culture, and it seemed like a company where I would not want to work. As I walked out, I thought about the previous times I had shopped there and how the workers seemed either beaten down or angry. Michelle and I have come to avoid the lines of certain checkers because they seem so angry and it's painful to interact with them. Their behavior now made more sense in light of the note.

The note caused me to think about how the owner has lost touch with the many worlds outside of his own. The worlds of his employees. The worlds of his customers. He didn't think about how the sign would appear to customers or to his staff. He didn't understand how the note was like a billboard regarding his company's culture. If he couldn't see this, it's likely he couldn't see what the culture is really like at the store or how his staff views the culture.

Not long ago I met some former colleagues for

drinks. The group now works in a variety of jobs at different companies. Our conversation turned to culture, and we had a wide-ranging conversation about what creates a good culture. Out of curiosity, I asked everyone to describe in one word the culture of his or her current organizations. The responses were eye-opening:

- individualistic (as opposed to team-oriented)
- masculine
- cutthroat
- lazy
- independent

Each person in our group clearly saw their firm's culture. It was obvious to them. Yet these dysfunctional cultures were not obvious to the people running their firms. Would any leader want to say they led a group whose culture is defined as lazy?

We have the opportunity to shape and create the culture. Our opportunities to do so are unlimited. For example, at my last firm, I gave everyone a small holiday gift along with a handwritten thank-you note. There were about one hundred people in the business, and it took me hours and hours to write something thoughtful and personal to each person. I generally got very little feedback on the notes but noticed that a few people put them up in their workspace. The notes were a way for me to show I cared about the people and appreciated their efforts.

The notes were also part of my deliberate effort to shape the culture to what we called a collegial culture. "Collegial" meant we cared for and about each other, we treated each other respectfully, and while individual accomplishments were valued, they could not come at the expense of another colleague's success.

The onboarding of new employees also proved to be a great place to shape our culture. Because this is where new employees would have their first experience with the firm, the process became a key focus for me. Prior to arriving at our firm, each new employee received in the mail a backpack with the name of our company on it and a handwritten note from me welcoming to them to the firm. During the first week of their employment, I would meet with each new employee and tell them about the history of our business, what we were seeking to accomplish, and what our culture was like. I also told them that as new employees they had the most clarity about what was wrong with our business. I encouraged them to speak up and question anything that didn't make sense. Finally, I would go to lunch with them within thirty days of their joining the firm. All of this intended to communicate that they were important and valued, and we needed them to contribute to the growth of the business.

Using this onboarding process, we sent a message about our culture even before new employees started work. Being part of the onboarding process forced me to continually focus on my own role in helping shape the culture. As a bonus, I got to meet each person when they joined, and that allowed me to connect with them going forward.

We have the opportunity to shape the culture of our organizations. We should act on these opportunities.

What is one word you use to describe your culture? Consider writing that word down. Then consider asking the people you work with for their words—you may have to allow for anonymous contributions. Hopefully no one will say "lazy" or "cutthroat," but you might get some insights into your culture.

And now you will have to excuse me while I write down a word . . .

Cowboy Jim

The first movie I saw in a theater was a western called *Shane*. I was five or six years old and crazy about cowboys. Dad took me to see *Shane* in a second-run movie theater in our town. In a family of seven children, it was always a big deal to do something alone with Dad. Despite the smell of stale popcorn and fraying seats, I was thrilled. I was going to a movie by myself with Dad, and it was a cowboy movie!

Shane made a huge impression on me. Filmed in the Grand Tetons near Jackson Hole, Wyoming, it showed vast, sweeping plains, with mountains jutting up in the background. For a boy living in a Chicago suburb, the landscape was otherworldly. Beyond the landscape, what made the movie so great was that it featured a small boy named Joey. Joey was around my age and, like me, he was awe struck by the gunfighter Shane, the tortured hero of the movie. Watching the movie, I saw it through Joey's eyes. We were two supporting actors, helping Shane fight the bad guys. For a long time afterwards, I refused to wear short pants because cowboys don't wear short pants.

I was thinking about Shane today while talking to someone who is returning to his old job. He has deep ties to his employer and coworkers, and is looking forward to returning. He is also feeling a bit of anxiety; would things be the same as before? We discussed the idea of how we are all starring in our own movie and how our movies are all about me, me, and me. We discussed how he might consider turning up at work not as the star in his own movie but playing a role in someone else's movie. This is not to say he would defer to others or be submissive but rather focus on connecting to others and helping them with their roles.

What does "starring in your own movie" mean? It means we are constantly thinking about how everyone else perceives us. We imagine ourselves in a spotlight where people are staring at us, judging us, and analyzing us. This causes us to make mistakes in our perception and judgment. We try too hard to impress or worry that everyone is looking at us. We end up feeling awkward and unsure of ourselves.

> The reality is everyone else is starring in his or her own movie too.

While they are immersed in their own roles and lines, we are just passing through as extras or supporting actors. All the things we worry about go unnoticed while everyone is busy making their own movies.

It's easy to think we are the stars of our own movies. After all, people look to us for advice, decisions, and insights. They analyze our dress and moods, trying to read us.

We control whether we are stars or supporting actors. While there are certainly times when we must be stars, there are also times when being supporting actors is appropriate. Being the supporting actor means connecting with the other person, understanding them, and helping them with their role.

At one job, I decided to leave when I realized I knew the name of my boss's spouse and children, the sports they played, the school they went to, and the challenges they were having in school. I also realized that if asked to name nearly anything about me, my boss would have no answer. Starring in his own movie, I was nothing more than a vague extra to him. Sure, we got along well and he was a nice guy, but it was time for me to move on.

When we choose to become supporting actors in someone else's movie, it means we are making the effort to give them our attention, to understand the things that are important to them. We connect. Rather than being on send, we are on receive.

Spoiler alert: at the end of *Shane*, Joey watches Shane ride out of the valley where Joey and his family live. It is dark, and Joey stands at the top of the mountain pass as Shane recedes into the darkness. "Come back, Shane! Shane, come back!" he calls, and the valley echoes with his small boy's voice: "Come back, Shane, Shane . . ."

When you take the time to be the supporting actor in someone else's movie, it's less likely they will ride off the way I did. And while Cowboy Jim eventually relented and began wearing short pants, I retain a fondness for chaps. It's too bad Michelle forbids me to wear them in either her movie or mine! And now you will excuse me while I see if *Shane* is on Netflix . . .

I Was Just
Trying to Help

"Aaargh! I have to go the bathroom," Michelle said.

Michelle and I were on a five-mile run during a cold day in December, and we still had to 2.5 miles to go before we got back home. One of the dirty little secrets about running is that it can bring on a sudden and powerful urge to use the bathroom. As a result, runners always keep an eye out for emergency bathrooms (thank you, Starbucks!).

"There is a bathroom a couple blocks ahead at a construction site," I said.

"I hate those porta-potties! They are always dirty, and it's cold out! Besides, I don't have to go that badly," said Michelle in an irritated tone of voice.

"I was just trying to help!" I thought, and we continued on in a frosty silence.

Our conversation was life-changing for me. In less than a minute, I came to understand something called the Drama Triangle. I learned about the Drama Triangle at a year-long leadership class at the Stagen Leadership Academy. The Drama Triangle was conceived by Dr. Steven Karpman, and argues that our default state is one of fear and anxiety. We then naturally use strategies to manage our fear and anxiety. These strategies are found in an upside-down triangle called the Drama Triangle. At the bottom of the triangle is the Victim, and at the top on either end of the triangle is the Rescuer and the Persecutor. Karpman defines the Victim, Rescuer, and Persecutor as follows:

The Victim: Passive, and blames other people or circumstances for their problems and anxiety

The Rescuer: Looks for Victims to rescue and wants the feeling of having saved the day

The Persecutor: The apparent cause of the Victim's problem

Suddenly aware of the Drama Triangle, I saw it everywhere, starting with myself. What was more astounding was how fast I could move through all three roles. Let me explain.

When Michelle announced she had a problem—needing to use the bathroom—she was acting as a Victim. When I jumped in with a solution, I was acting as the Rescuer. Because my advice was unasked for and unwelcome, she responded with irritation, and I became the Persecutor. When I had my feelings hurt because my advice was rejected, I became a Victim. In sixty seconds, I went from Rescuer to Persecutor to Victim. Wow.

Now let's examine how the Drama Triangle can show up at the office. Imagine you supervise a cross-functional team working on a critical project. As a good manager, you regularly meet with your direct reports for one-on-one meetings. Just before lunch, you meet with Pat, who tells you the critical project is behind schedule, largely due to Kevin (who also reports to you) not keeping his commitments. After lunch, you have your one-on-one with Kevin and ask him about Pat's feedback. Kevin erupts and tells you Pat is a Machiavellian backstabber who is constantly seeking to undermine him. You don't know who to believe and aren't sure what to do. On your way home, you get a text from your boss, who bumped into Kevin in the hall and wants to know why the team isn't getting along and why the project is behind. Upon arriving home, you spend the next hour telling your partner all about your bad day.

In this example, Pat was the Victim, passively telling you about his problem and casting Kevin as his Persecutor. Not one to let problems fester, you jumped in as Pat's Rescuer. When you spoke to Kevin about it, you became his Persecutor. And when you got home and verbally threw up all over your partner, you became the Victim.

What's a person to do? In the next essay, we will learn how to escape the Drama Triangle.

I Was Just Trying to Help: Part Two

As a leader or manager, you continually face problems. Often you are judged on how quickly you solve these problems so that you can get more problems to solve. You are on a hamster wheel, and it feels quite good because you are making it go around and around really quickly. During my career, I worked for a company headquartered in London. Since I live in Chicago, the London office was six hours ahead. Every morning I woke up to an inbox full of emails from my London colleagues. As a response, I began waking up in the middle of the night, checking my email and firing off responses. I wanted to make the hamster wheel spin even faster, and by working in the middle of the night, I thought I was demonstrating I was both committed and responsive.

In the prior essay, I wrote about the Drama Triangle, a model with an upside-down triangle describing how we engage with problems out of anxiety and fear. The Triangle has a Victim at the bottom and Rescuer and Persecutor at the top. Our challenge in life is to identify and then escape the Drama Triangle. How do we do this?

In his book *The Power of TED* (*The Empowerment Dynamic*),[25] David Emerald Womeldorff has created a second triangle called the TED Triangle. The triangle is right side up and has a Creator at the top and a Coach and Challenger at the bottom corners of the triangle. These roles are defined as follows:

> **The Creator:** the opposite of the Victim. Rather than being problem-oriented, the Creator asks, "What do I want?" or "What outcome do I want?"

> **The Coach:** Opposite of the Rescuer. The Coach is a Creator who sees others as fellow Creators. The Coach seeks to help other Creators clarify their outcomes or define the steps required to reach their outcomes.

> **The Challenger:** The opposite of the Persecutor. The Challenger, as defined by Womeldorff, "is focused on learning and growth, holding a Creator accountable while encouraging learning, action, and next steps."[26]

Our challenge is to see others as Creators and not as Victims. This means not taking on the Rescuer and Persecutor roles. Instead, it means learning to become a thoughtful questioner seeking to help fellow Creators understand their desired outcomes.

---

25 David Emerald Womeldorff, *The Power of TED*: The Empowerment Dynamic* (Bainbridge Island, WA: Polaris Publishing, 2016).

26 David Emerald Womeldorff, *The Power of TED*: The Empowerment Dynamic* (Bainbridge Island, WA: Polaris Publishing, 2016), p. 100–115.

It means helping them define the steps to achieve their outcomes.

In Womeldorff's thinking, we escape the Drama Triangle by shifting into the TED Triangle. This means 1) spotting a drama triangle, 2) pausing to reflect on what outcome you want, and then 3) shifting into the TED Triangle.

Let's examine how this can work in the real world. In my example from the prior essay, Michelle announced she had to go the bathroom, and I jumped in as a Rescuer. My rescue attempt irritated her, and she saw me as a Persecutor. When she pushed back on my rescue attempt, my feelings were hurt, and I became a Victim. Instead, I could have done the following:

1) Spotted my own instinct to jump in as the Rescuer. If I had stopped myself and made a shift, I might have said to myself, "You are about to become a Rescuer. Shift to being a Creator. What outcome do you want?" I would have said, "I want to understand Michelle's problem and what she thinks the solution is." I then could have gone into a Coach role and asked Michelle some clarifying questions, such as:

- How badly do you have to go?
- What is it you want to do about the problem?
- Can you make it home, or should we find a place to stop?

By treating Michelle as a Creator and not as a Victim, I allow her to define her outcome.

Here are some real-world tips for escaping the Drama Triangle:

- Start with yourself. Practice catching yourself in Victim mode. Anytime you are complaining, you are being a Victim. Someone asked me how my life would be different if I had known about the Drama Triangle years ago. I answered that I didn't know, but I did know I would have spent a lot less time complaining. Avoiding complaining is a useful behavior for us both personally and professionally. When we complain, we bring down the team's morale and send a message that complaining is an acceptable behavior within the team culture.

- Watch for yourself acting as the Rescuer. Anytime you jump in to solve a problem or take a problem from someone else, you are acting as the Rescuer. Remind yourself that while it feels good to be a Rescuer, you are not helping the Victim to become a Creator. By encouraging people on the team to bring you their problems, you prevent them from growing and becoming Creators.

- Don't tell someone they are being a Victim. Speaking from personal experience, it does not go down well! As my Stagen teacher Cindy noted, telling someone they are a Victim automatically makes you the Persecutor.

- Challenge yourself to find one instance a week where you got caught in the Drama Triangle, and one instance where you were able to make the shift to the TED Triangle. This will help you learn to make the shift to the TED Triangle.

- Be patient. You can't see the movie, buy the t-shirt, and be done with the Drama Triangle. It goes on forever; it's part of the human condition and a lifelong challenge for us.

- Teach it. If your team understands the Drama Triangle, asking them what outcome they want becomes a powerful tool for you and them.

And now you will excuse me; I've got some shifting to do . . .

Solitaire Leadership

As leaders, we face a tension between doing too much and doing too little. Sometimes our people want us to be more hands-on, and sometimes they wish we would back off. As with much of leadership, there are no easy answers.

As part of an assignment, I spent half a day listening to the key employees of a bank. I was there to get feedback on their CEO, Ike. I learned a lot and so did Ike. The feedback that was most surprising to me was about autonomy. The team felt Ike gave them too much autonomy at times. Although they appreciated his confidence in them, sometimes they wanted Ike's guidance on how he might approach the problems they were struggling with. This surprised me because generally people want more autonomy. In Ike's case, however, he had done such a good job giving them autonomy that his staff felt he had gone too far.

The team's feedback about autonomy illustrates the eternal tension we face. On the one hand, we come to work every day anxious to add value. We sometimes feel adrift if we aren't busy doing something. We encourage our staff to bring us problems, and we find our purpose in staying busy, solving problems, and feeling needed. We also might feel the need to justify our position, our title, and our compensation and seek to be seen doing something, no matter how trivial.

On the other hand, is it realistic to think we know how to do everyone's jobs better than they do? Shouldn't we get out of the way and let people do their work and be available on the infrequent occasions when they need our help? As the CEO of the bank learned, this is a balance that is difficult to get just right.

We often err on the side of activity and of trying to add value. Sometimes, however, our efforts to add value can backfire and have long-lasting effects.

Although it's hard to imagine today, there was a time during the late 1990s when personal computers were just entering the workplace. It was common for them to be shipped with the game of solitaire installed on them. Naturally, some people used their computers to play solitaire when they were bored or taking a break. During this time, Alan, the CEO of the investment company where I was working, saw an employee playing solitaire on her computer. Because he believed everyone should be working hard at all times, he became enraged at seeing her playing solitaire. To remedy this, he immediately ordered the IT department to remove solitaire from everyone's machines. I don't remember all the details, but I remember it was a difficult task and took up a lot of time and attention.

To me, removing solitaire seemed silly. Playing solitaire was not the problem. Playing solitaire might be a symptom of people not having enough work or of being lazy or taking a break, but solitaire was not the problem.

Alan's response to solitaire caused several problems. By removing the game, he sent a message to the company that said, "I don't trust you to manage your time and your work." When he went directly to the IT department rather than giving the problem to his direct reports, he demonstrated he didn't trust them. Finally, by getting involved with a minor issue, he sent a message that he was incapable of only focusing on the critical things that would help the firm prosper.

Alan's response had unintended consequences on the company's culture. Knowing Alan didn't trust them created a mutual lack of trust and respect between the employees and Alan. Fear also became part of the culture. People were afraid of being perceived as not working or not being hardworking. So people invested a lot of time pretending to be working, at least when Alan was around.

There was yet another problem with the solitaire incident. It demonstrated that neither Alan nor the employees understood each other. Alan felt he was making the company more productive by stomping out solitaire. The staff, on the other hand, felt they were being persecuted, perhaps for the sins of one person.

We see ourselves as problem-solvers and like the feeling that comes from solving problems. We like to feel we are making things better and accomplishing things. We like to feel we are making a difference. If we see something wrong, we want to jump in and fix it. Despite this emotional need, the reality is we likely only do a few things each year that make a difference. Everything else might be administratively and technically necessary, but it doesn't make a difference in the fortunes of the business.

The challenge is knowing
those few things that truly
make a difference.

There is no easy answer for discerning the few, critical things you should work on as if your hair were on fire. You may not know until next year or years from now. In the meantime, you can self-audit. Are you policing the solitaire games of your world? Or are you working on things that, if accomplished, would make an enormous difference in the business? And now you will excuse me while I play some solitaire on my vintage 1997 Compaq . . .

Me vs. Me

Two years ago at Christmas, Maggie and Connor gave me a framed quote by Marcus Aurelius. It says, "Be tolerant with others and strict with yourself." This is my favorite quote and the North Star that I try to follow in living my life as a person and as a leader. Let me explain.

The first part of the quote, "Be tolerant of others," reminds me to work on turning off my inner critic. I often catch myself criticizing someone else, either in my mind or in a conversation. Being critical of others sets a bad example and makes those with whom I am speaking wonder if I criticize them as well. I ask myself if what the other person is doing is something I have ever done? Inevitably the answer is yes, I have done the same thing. How can I criticize someone for doing the same thing I have done? Since I don't control the behavior of others, why spend time thinking and talking about what he or she is doing?

The second part of the quote, "strict with yourself," also has multiple meanings. It reminds me to hold myself accountable for being tolerant of others and not getting caught up in cataloging the faults of others. It also inspires me to continue working on myself and developing as a person and a leader. I aspire to be strict with myself in pushing myself to grow and get better. I aspire to stay in my own lane, working on my own faults since those are the only ones in my control. Marcus's simple eight words of wisdom are a continual call to work on my self-development.

As I work on being "strict with myself," I have found a deeper meaning as well. I call this "Me vs. Me."

Everything comes down to this. Not biting my nails, giving up sugar, listening well, thinking about the other person's perspective, not looking at my phone every three minutes—it's all a struggle to control myself. Whatever I want to stop doing, whatever I want to start doing, it's all up to me.

I am an intensely competitive person. Over time, I have focused on competing with myself, creating Me vs. Me challenges such as doing one hundred burpees every day for a year or running a hundred-mile race. I wrote earlier about the Drama Triangle, a concept that takes us out of being a Victim, Rescuer, or Persecutor and into being a Coach, Challenger, or Creator. Part of the appeal of the Drama Triangle for me is its ongoing challenge. Can I catch myself before starting to whine like a Victim? Can I be a Creator?

Sometimes it seems so simple to be disciplined and win the Me vs. Me contest. I would like to lose ten pounds. Just eat less! Yet I struggle. Me vs. Me. It's a constant winning and losing. Sometimes it's discouraging when I observe people like the ex-Navy SEAL Jocko Willink whose motto is "discipline equals freedom." He is up at 4:30 a.m. doing a punishing workout, and if he is traveling and can't squeeze in a workout, he knocks out one hundred burpees in his hotel room. It would be great if I had that discipline. The battle, though, is not with Jocko or to become

Jocko. The battle is to become who I want to be.

My personal competitions, while intensely challenging, are in a sense easy. It's easy to pick out a physical challenge and chase after it. The real challenge is to see myself accurately and work on my behaviors moment to moment, day after day, being honest with myself about success and failure.

Seeing myself accurately is a challenge. Sometimes I am too tough on myself and get stuck in imposter syndrome. Other times I am too much a knower, full of unsolicited advice and solutions.

Me vs. Me is a lifelong challenge. Some days I wish I could leave it behind, and on other days it's all I can think about. Me vs. Me is the joy of living, the joy of the journey, never quite arriving but always pushing to do things where I am challenged and may fail. And I have failed often. While engaged in my year-long burpee challenge, I did one-hundred burpees after finishing marathons and as late as eleven p.m. in my hotel room after a long, boozy dinner. I stuck with it. But in the end, I missed days 364 and 365 when I was unable to overcome a violent stomach flu. At the time, I was upset about failing, but looking back now, I see all the days when I had to find the mental strength to do the burpees. And although I failed, I learned I had it in me to do something difficult.

It's easy to avoid Me vs. Me. It's seductive to believe you have it all figured out and to defend your position, your status, or whatever you think is important. It's seductive to think you know it all and you are a mini-god to whom everyone should defer. It's seductive to never test yourself or ask, "What if I am wrong?"

To avoid being surprised and finding that suddenly you don't have it all figured out, it helps to think about what might go wrong. The Stoics called this *premeditatio malorum*, which is the process of thinking about what could go wrong or what could be lost. After my boss lost his job abruptly, I kept his name tag on my credenza as a daily premeditatio malorum of how someday I could lose my job. It was a powerful reminder to never take my job for granted.

The same thinking can be applied to our own behaviors. By asking ourselves questions like the ones below, we progress on our journey of challenging ourselves.

- What did I do wrong today?
- How could I have done better?
- What do I aspire to, and am I making progress toward those aspirations?
- Where might I be wrong?
- Do I really know what I think I know?
- Can I prove I know what I know?

Can you get better as a leader? I don't know the answer—only you do. I know I can . . . and now you will have to excuse me while I do a few burpees . . .

Chasing the Sale

While looking for prospective business partners, I met a consultant who travels a lot for work. We were grumbling about traveling, and he told me the following story.

A member of his team had been working on closing a large piece of business. The team member kept insisting he needed his boss to travel to the prospect's office for a final meeting where his boss could help close the sale. While his boss was supportive, the prospect was located in Switzerland, and the boss felt a nine-hour flight from Chicago was a long way to travel for a short meeting. "Is it critical I be there?" he asked. "Yes," said the team member. "I need you to be there to meet with the prospect's senior person. Unless you two guys meet, we won't close the sale." "Okay," the boss said, and slung himself onto a plane and turned up at the meeting in Switzerland. Introduced to the senior person he was there to meet, he started with some small talk: "Where do you live?" he asked. The senior person responded by naming a suburb in a Chicago just a short drive from the consultant's Chicago office. The consultant had flown nine hours to meet someone who lived a half an hour from his office.

This story is rich in lessons for me. In my Stagen leadership class, we learned about the Drama Triangle. As part of overcoming the Drama Triangle, we seek to develop a habit of asking ourselves, "What outcome do I want?" Asking this question has almost unlimited application. In this instance, the consultant could have begun by asking himself what outcome he wanted. Presumably, it would have been to help his colleague close a large account without flying to Switzerland. If he asked his colleague to brainstorm on how to accomplish this, they might have discovered that the senior person he needed to meet lived and worked nearby.

Closely linked to asking "What outcome do I want?" is asking the right question. It's easy to get locked into seeing the issue from just one perspective and then solving for the issue from that perspective. When we get locked in, it's hard to ask the right questions. In the case of the consultant, both he and his colleague became locked into the perspective that a meeting in Switzerland meant the participants lived in Switzerland.

We can look a lot like the consultants when we get locked into a perspective. For example, Michelle and I were walking through a nearby neighborhood on our way to dinner. It was windy as we walked by a house, when we heard a strange sound. We determined the sound was coming from a backup generator, and I guessed the generator was going through a brief weekly start-up test. A couple of blocks later, we heard a second generator. "All the backup generators must be programmed to test themselves at five p.m. every Saturday," I said to Michelle.

Returning home after dinner in the dark, we realized the power was out in the neighborhood. The generators were running not because of a test but because there was no power! Because I didn't know the power was out in the neighborhood, I had come up with my own story about why two generators would be running at the same time. I didn't ask myself if there might be another reason two generators were running at the same time. Ignoring that it had been windy, I blocked out the fact that high winds sometimes cause downed power lines.

This is a minor example of locking into a view. We have to forever guard against our instincts to quickly reach conclusions and decisions.

> Slowing down, asking what outcome we want, and looking carefully at the facts will help us become better problem-solvers.

And avoid long trips! And now you will have to excuse me while I cancel a trip . . .

Sunk-Cost Bias: My Three-Year Mistake

On my first day of law school, I turned up for class in my college uniform: Chuck Taylor high tops, perfectly torn jeans, and a Jackson Browne t-shirt that went perfectly with my full beard and full head of hair (glory days!). I didn't know a lot about law school or why I wanted to be a lawyer other than that it seemed like lawyers read a lot, and I really liked reading.

By my second semester I realized I wasn't going to be a good lawyer; yes, there was a lot of reading, but there was also a lot of writing, and much of it was technical and detailed. My classmates were hypercompetitive and smart and very career-focused, whereas I was not. My jeans and t-shirts were at odds with the upper-class students who were clerking at law firms and wearing dresses and suits and ties (this was before business casual hit the workplace). I was also learning that the practice of law was highly specialized; students picked an area of focus, sort of like picking a major, and tried to find a job clerking at a law firm that focused on their specialty. And I hated all of it because I knew at some level it wasn't for me.

So what did I do? I stole some of Dad's old suits (looking straight out of *Mad Men* a couple decades too soon), started working thirty hours a week at a commercial real estate company while taking night classes, and, after three mediocre years, graduated from law school. I had school loans and no job and didn't try very hard to get a job as a lawyer. When the real estate company offered me a job running the lease administration department, I gladly took it and never looked back.

My law school experience is a painful example of something called sunk-cost bias. Having decided to go to law school, I refused to walk away from my commitment even though I quickly knew practicing law wasn't for me. By not walking away, I gave up three years of income and took on a lot of school loans. Worse, I gave up three years of my life doing something I wasn't enjoying.

> Sunk-cost bias occurs when we continue with a course of action or investment because of our aversion to loss.

In my case, I was averse to admitting becoming a lawyer was a mistake. I stubbornly persisted because emotionally it was easier to continue on instead of admitting my mistake. It's useful to understand how sunk-cost bias can show up in our world:

- **Strategy:** we choose a strategy for our business, and it isn't working. Rather than admit failure, we redouble our efforts and work harder and spend more money in hopes the strategy will become successful.

- **People:** we make a bad hire, and rather than admit we made a mistake, we ignore their underperformance or make excuses for them or otherwise invest in them while the little voice in our head says it's not going to work.

- **Emotions:** we make a mistake, and someone calls us out on it. Rather than admitting our mistake, we double down and invest emotion and mental energy in rationalizing why we are right.

How can we avoid sunk-cost bias? It's not easy but it begins with taking an inventory of what's not going well. As you study what's not going well, you might see that some things would improve with more attention while other things are never going to get better.

For example, in June 2014, Amazon released its Fire Phone. Intended to compete with the Android and iPhone, it was bundled with a free year of Amazon Prime. As the Fire Phone sales got off to slow start, Amazon dropped the price several times. The phone continued selling poorly, however, and in August 2015 Amazon discontinued it.

Amazon's response to the poor sales of the Fire Phone is a good example of avoiding sunk-cost bias. Within fourteen months of launching the phone, it had killed the business and taken a $170 million write-down. This must have been painful for Amazon and was certainly a very visible failure. Yet it went forward, took the pain, and moved on.

When we are willing write off unsuccessful commitments or investments, we go through pain to admit we were wrong. The alternative, however, is to ignore our bias, escalate our commitment, and experience greater pain in the end.

And now you will excuse me while I go to my continuing ed course to keep my law license current . . .

Going into Debt

During 1999 there was a lot of fear about something called "Y2K." Y2K was a programming problem that arose during the 1960s and 1970s. Due to the need to save storage space at the time, programmers abbreviated dates by dropping the first two digits of a year, so that "1978" was written as "78." As the millennium approached in 1999, there was widespread fear that computer programs would read the abbreviation of 2000 ("00") as the year 1900. The result would be the failure of critical computer systems across a variety of industries. Much money and effort were expended during 1999 to prevent systems from failing, but when the clock struck midnight, there were few issues.

Y2K is a good example in software development of something called "technical debt." Technical debt arises when a programming problem is addressed but not in such a way that the problem is permanently resolved. Although the problem has been fixed for the short term, the fix leaves significantly more work and expense for the future, thereby creating the technical debt.

Technical debt is just one type of debt we may face. There are other types of debt, such as difficult employee debt, difficult customer debt, and cash cow debt. Often it is not easy to get out of debt.

Difficult employee debt happens when we put off dealing with difficult people. Generally, putting off dealing with a difficult employee ends badly. For example, I am aware of a small-business owner who hired a friend as his CFO. On the basis of their friendship, the owner gave the CFO very little oversight. The CFO proved to be a better friend than accountant, however, and the business suffered significant financial problems when the CFO did not file tax returns for the business.

Difficult customers can also create debt and can be tough to "fire," particularly if they represent a significant amount of the firm's revenues. A friend told me about a firm with a difficult customer. The customer routinely shouted at and verbally abused the firm's employees. Learning of this, the owner of the firm fired the customer and accepted the resulting financial pain because it was the right thing to do within his firm's culture. The founder of the firm chose short-term pain over incurring longer-term debt. In this case, the longer-term debt might have been losing good employees who couldn't work with the customer as well as possibly becoming financially dependent on a difficult customer.

Cash cow debt occurs when the most profitable part of a business prevents the business from diversifying and instead forces the company's profits to be reinvested back into the cash cow portion of the business. I began my career working at a real estate company that sold syndicated real estate products. At the time, there was a strong demand for such products because of their tax benefits. As a result, the syndication business was highly profitable and a "cash cow" for the company. Wisely, the firm took some of their profits and diversified into other products and lines of business. This decision was not fully embraced by those in the syndication business because it meant less money was being invested in their business.

When the tax code changed several years later, the deductions fueling the syndication business were eliminated. Suddenly there was little demand for syndicated real estate products. The firm I worked for survived because they had diversified and refused to go into debt with their cash cow. Other competitors that had not diversified were forced to sell or close down altogether. Choosing to stick with their cash cow business had been good in the short term but left them heavily indebted in the long term.

Sometimes we can't avoid going into debt.

Perhaps we need the difficult customer for the business to survive. Perhaps the business isn't strong enough to harvest profits from the cash cow portion of the business. In these cases, we have to be honest with ourselves about the debt we are incurring and how we intend to get out of debt in the future.

While going into debt is easy, getting out can be tougher: just ask all the firms that spent millions in 1999 to prepare for Y2K. And now you will have to excuse me while I throw away my Y2K survival kit . . .

Getting Out of My Own Way

When I heard that my former boss named Andrew had lost his job, it caused me to reflect on our time together. He had worked at the firm for twenty years and led it out of some difficult times. Andrew sat four thousand miles away from me in the firm's London headquarters. Initially, this seemed as if it would be a bad thing, but I found I liked the autonomy and the freedom of not seeing my boss every day. I also found it led to various communication challenges.

Andrew was from Australia, living in the UK, and I was located in the US, and we initially struggled to communicate with each other. We came from different cultures, which had different business and legal practices, and these differences came between us at times.

I began reporting to Andrew when I was unexpectedly promoted. I hadn't sought the job and didn't know Andrew. I thought I was a stopgap person, only there until he found someone he liked better. This led to a low level of trust on my part.

In my Stagen leadership class, we learned that this behavior is called "telling ourselves a story." I had looked at the facts and come up with a story about what they meant. Because I didn't ask Andrew about this story I was telling myself, we were not on the same page about why I had been promoted. Years later, when I learned the real story, I regretted not discussing it with Andrew.

Over time, I learned what Andrew wanted around communication. He wanted no surprises, good or bad. The worst thing that could happen was for him not to know something. I learned what he needed to know and how to communicate effectively with him. Here, too, I made things more difficult by not asking Andrew for feedback and instead relying on trial and error.

Over time, I also came to understand Andrew's expectations. They were pretty simple: grow the business, control expenses, and manage the team. What took me longer to understand was that Andrew had invested me with authority and power. He expected me to use it wisely to grow and manage the business. He saw more clearly than I did the power that came with my title. By telling myself that I was an interim replacement, I couldn't see my authority. Like the texts between Michelle and I, it was a case of two people looking at the same thing and coming to a different conclusion.

My lack of understanding of Andrew's support and my blind spot for the power of the role also showed up in how I worked with our home office. Home offices and regional offices often have tensions in how they work together. The home office worries about what the regional office is doing and seeks tight oversight. In turn, the regional office finds the home office full of ad hoc requests and bureaucracy that strangles the growth of the region. It's easy in these circumstances for the people in the region to see themselves as heroes who were not only growing the business but doing so despite the blocking efforts of home office. I was that guy for a long time. Only when I understood we couldn't succeed without the people in the home office, who were incredibly talented and hardworking, did we begin to work well together.

My breakthroughs were gradual and incremental. I began to understand my title came with authority and power, and I began to use it appropriately. I developed a deep appreciation for my colleagues in home office, and came to understand our success in the US depended on a strong working relationship with our UK colleagues. I worked hard to connect both groups and help us each understand the other.

Looking back, I can see how I struggled in my own head and blocked myself from doing my best. It wasn't Andrew or the home office getting in my way; it was the stories I was telling myself.

> When we show our people that we believe in them and help them learn new stories, we rise to our highest levels.

Thank you, Andrew!

And now you will have to excuse while I try and figure out what it means when someone in the UK says, "It's like chalk and cheese" . . .

Self-Interest or Self-Delusion? The Eternal Challenge of Leadership

The easiest and hardest thing for us to understand is self-interest. Self-interest has three components: 1) understanding our own self-interest and avoiding self-delusion; 2) understanding the self-interest of others; and 3) a willingness to revise your views based on feedback from the external world. This essay focuses on 1) understanding our own self-interest.

Do we really know what we want? We certainly think we do. We are easily fooled, however. For example, I received a speeding ticket about three hours from my home. To avoid having the ticket go on my driving record, I had to appear in court at a later date. This required taking a day off of work and spending more than six hours driving to and from the courthouse. While it seemed that saving a few minutes by speeding was what I wanted, it was not in my self-interest to spend a day traveling to the courthouse a few weeks later. Had I more thoughtfully considered my self-interest, I might have decided to drive at the speed limit and avoid risking receiving a speeding ticket. Although I had considered my short-term interest—get home slightly more quickly—I hadn't considered my longer-term interest of what would happen if I received a speeding ticket—spending a day driving to and from a courthouse.

We do well to consider our self-interest across time scales, as well as consider the interests of the firm, and the interests of our team and our relationships with the team. For example, if you get what you want and the other person does not, how will your relationship be in the future? If you get what you want and the company does not, how does it impact the company?

A consultant who was hired to save a small business told me during his engagement he had to fire the company's top salesperson. Why? The salesperson had acted in his self-interest by convincing the owner of the business to pay him a commission schedule so rich that it brought the firm to the brink of bankruptcy. For the salesperson, he got his self-interest right in the short term because he received higher commissions. But when it led to his being fired, it was not in his long-term self-interest. He was fired because by acting in his short-term self-interest, he had badly damaged the company.

Fully understanding what you want requires taking into account a wide range of factors and arriving at a conclusion about what your self-interest should be. Sometimes you may have to act against your self-interest to serve the best interests of the firm or your team. This is not easy, and it's against our primal instincts.

When you grasp how complicated your own self-interest can be, you can begin to see how this applies equally to others.

My next essay will cover understanding the self-interest of others. And now you will excuse me while I go pay a speeding ticket . . .

My Own Personal Blindside

In my last essay, I wrote about understanding our own self-interest and how we can fool ourselves. We can also fool ourselves that we fully understand the self-interest of others. Not being fooled is one of our toughest assignments. While it is logical and rational to seek to understand another person's self-interest, we often fail to do this. I like to think I am particularly good at thinking about the self-interest of others, but I am often humbled how often I get it wrong.

A few months ago, my adult daughter Christine texted me. Would Michelle and I be at home this coming weekend, she wondered. I was happy about her text because I enjoy spending time with my Christine; she is upbeat and fun and leaves a little sunshine wherever she goes. I assumed from her text that she wanted to spend a few hours with us. Christine lives a full and busy life, and we are always grateful for any time we have together with her. Since we planned to be away for the coming weekend, I texted my daughter that we should try and find a different time. "Okay," she said. "I want to stop by and pick up my birthday present."

Wow! I didn't see that coming! Since it was in my self-interest to assume my daughter wanted to spend a few hours with us, I hadn't considered she was planning a pop-in visit to pick up her present. Although I was disappointed that we wouldn't see much of my daughter, I was aghast at how badly I had read the situation. I had let my own self-interest block me from considering my daughter's self-interest. Unable to put myself in her shoes, I had never considered her busy life and any of the reasons she might be coming to visit.

My daughter's text made me wonder: if I couldn't accurately see the self-interest of my twenty-five-year-old daughter, how accurately was I seeing the self-interest of others? By thinking only about myself, I had violated one of Stephen's Covey's *The 7 Habits of Highly Effective People*: "Seek first to understand, then to be understood."[27]

How do we teach ourselves to think about the self-interest of others? It begins with asking yourself whether you have sought to understand the other person. If you were in their shoes, what would you want? Have you tested for this understanding? Are you aware of the biases and lenses that you are using to look at the other person? Could you explain the other person's self-interest to a six-year-old?

The paradox of seeking to understand someone else's self-interest is that it's easier to get what you want if you know what the other person wants.

27 Stephen R. Covey, *The 7 Habits of Highly Effective People: Powerful Lessons in Personal Change* (New York: Simon & Schuster, 2004), p. 249.

In other words, your own self-interest begins with fully understanding the other person's self-interest.

If it's good practice to understand another's self-interest, why then do we struggle? In part, it's because we are self-centered and selfish and spend all day thinking about ourselves. Acting on our self-interest is what we do. Thinking about someone else's self-interest is unnatural and feels awkward.

Understanding another's self-interest is also made more difficult by our tech tools, which rob us of voice and sight while encouraging speed. It is easy to fall into a rhythm of fast responses to emails and texts and slip into a self-centered mind set without taking the time to understand what the other person really wants.

If I had been thinking about Christine's self-interest, my thinking might have gone something like this: "Hmmmm . . . she is usually quite busy and pressed for time. When pressed for time, she usually blocks out an hour or two that would work for her to visit with us. But she hasn't suggested blocking out some time. What might that mean?" I also might have asked myself, "When I was 25, where did I want to be? Anywhere but with my parents! Therefore, might it be possible she would like her visit to be as short as possible?"

I don't have any silver bullets to fix this because there aren't any. It's hard to think about what someone else wants. It requires intention and going slower than we may prefer. What's even harder, however, is to ask ourselves if we are wrong as I was with Christine.

"What if I am wrong?" How often do we really consider this question? And now you will excuse me; I have to run out and get Christine's birthday present . . .

Loving Being Wrong

In my last two essays, I touched on understanding our own self-interest as well as that of others. In this essay, I discuss how we should understand that it is in our self-interest to seek out where we are wrong. In my last essay, I wrote about my daughter Christine texting me to see if Michelle and I would be at home over the weekend. While I was certain her text meant she wanted to spend a few hours with us, Christine was only stopping by to collect her birthday present. In hindsight, I had been wrong about why Christine was coming to visit and blinded by my self-interest.

There are many models of leadership. One of the dominant leadership models is the all-knowing leader. Think of the Wizard of Oz sitting behind his curtain or Henry Ford who is supposed to have said, "If I had asked people what they wanted, they would have said faster horses." Although there is some debate about whether Ford actually spoke these words, the legend arose because of his conviction that he knew what was best for the customer. It's easy to think of an all-knowing leader as someone who always knows the right way forward.

The truth is no one can be right all the time. It is also true most of us do not enjoy being wrong or having our errors be highly visible. We often spend a lot of time making sure we are perceived as being correct. At a conference, I heard a speaker claim he had made four hundred correct predictions regarding companies and business trends. Clearly, he believed it was in his self-interest to be perceived as always being correct.

We should go beyond recognizing we can be wrong on occasion. We should understand it's in our self-interest to wire ourselves to continually learn where we are wrong. This is what Marc Andreessen, the founder of Netscape and now a venture capitalist, calls "strong opinions loosely held." Rather than protecting our egos, we are looking for the bad news or the facts that don't fit our worldview. We recognize it's in our self-interest to know when we are wrong and change our mind when the facts change.

How do people wire themselves to learn when they are wrong? The great strategist John Boyd called this looking for mismatches. A mismatch is something that does not match your prior expectations. For example, if the weather forecast was for a sunny day and you hear thunder, the thunder is a mismatch. By choosing to change your mind and find an umbrella, you will stay dry. But if you choose to ignore the mismatch and go outside without an umbrella, you will be caught in the thunderstorm you chose to ignore.

History is full of examples of ignored mismatches. BlackBerry and Nokia scoffed at the first version of the iPhone and responded too late when the threat was obvious. Hitler did not respond immediately to the Allied D-Day landings in Normandy with overwhelming force. Closed to the facts that didn't fit his view that the main invasion force would land elsewhere, he was too late in responding.

In my own life, I have ignored mismatches, including becoming lost during a trail marathon. Blocking out the lack of other runners, it wasn't until I had run a mile or two in the wrong direction that I was forced to admit I was lost. That was a long race!

Self-interest is multilayered and nuanced. It is more like a language that is difficult to speak and understand. We are all speaking our own self-interest dialects and often fail to understand what we are saying or what others are saying. We should reflect on these multiple layers of self-interest. When you understand your self-interest lies not in keeping score but rather in continually trying to see the world accurately, you go beyond self-interest and arrive at the truth. And now you will excuse me while I go change my mind . . .

James and the Baby Unicorn

The result of some minor outpatient surgery left me with a large white bandage on my forehead. Under the bandage was a bulky pressure bandage giving me the appearance of having an egg growing out of my forehead. I looked like a baby unicorn. After arriving home, Michelle and I went out to eat and I kept my hat on in the restaurant.

Observing myself, I tried to understand why I was hiding my bandage. I came up with a few reasons:

- I was embarrassed at looking like a baby unicorn.
- I didn't want people asking what happened.
- I didn't want to appear weak.

I was a bit disappointed in myself. Wasn't I mentally strong enough to not care what other people thought? Wasn't I strong enough to ignore other people's looks? Watching my behavior, I had to admit fitting in was a more powerful force than I would have been willing to acknowledge.

To be or not to be a unicorn is a challenge for us. On the one hand, we want to do the right things, even when that means going against what the team thinks.

On the other hand, doing what we believe is the right thing when everyone else disagrees with us can make us feel as if we are sprouting a horn out of our forehead.

What's the right way forward? There is no easy answer. As always, it begins with knowing ourselves and being objective about our own preferred style and behaviors. Do we care about being liked at all costs, or are we willing to go it alone for something we feel strongly about? If we go it alone, what are the likely consequences? Can we admit later that we were wrong if in fact it turns out we were wrong? Can we avoid saying "I told you so" if we were right?

We also have to ask ourselves if it's a minor or major decision. If it's a minor one, perhaps it's better to listen to others and preserve your voice for a major issue. How important is the issue to others? Might it be possible that it's minor to us and major to others?

> Leadership is lonely. While facing tough decisions, we have to consider how lonely we are we willing to be.

Can we stick it out if everyone shuns us? Or are we going to concede to the views of others if disagreeing means we will become outcasts?

Early in my career I took over a team with a track record of consistently missing its targets. We were preparing to take the business public, and I walked them through what would happen if our past performance had occurred while we were publicly traded. I framed the discussion around how public markets respond to underperformance, touching on how our share price would have fallen, how stock options would have become worthless, and how some of us would have lost our jobs. My message was ignored by much of the team. I found myself a pariah, perceived as a harsh critic. Despite our efforts, we were unable to take the business public and had to wind down the business. Over a few months we all went our different ways, and that was the end of the business.

Could I have found another way to present the message? Sure. And if I had to do it again, I would work harder to reach the team. But I would still play the critic and be honest about our underperformance. And I would still wear the loneliness of coming to work each day and being on the outside, of not being accepted. It was really a matter of asking myself what was the right thing to do for the business and for the team.

In the end, we all lost our jobs. But my decision to take the lonely path and become a unicorn was a big step in my journey as a leader. And now you will have to excuse me while I remove this giant bandage . . .

Authentic or Auto-Tune?

Not many people can see into the future, but Alan Lomax did. Lomax and his father John made thousands of field recordings of musicians around the world, including many in the South. They foresaw the widespread access to radio and realized it would kill off regional music. The Lomaxes set out to record as much music as they could before the regional variations were lost. From songs of the Mississippi Delta to folk songs from Europe to songs sung by prisoners on road gangs, Lomax captured a world quickly fading away. On his field recording of Mississippi Fred McDowell and his sister Fanny Davis, the listener hears Davis blowing on a kazoo wrapped in toilet paper. The sound is eerie and otherworldly and at times nearly drowns out McDowell's singing. It is raw and real and anything but perfect. While the music may not be for everyone, it has a purity that comes through.

Fast-forwarding to today, we live in a world where reality can be altered and cleaned up so as to present perfection. The use of Auto-Tune, a software used to correct slightly off-tune vocal performances, has created a body of music that is technically perfect.

Auto-Tune has become so embedded and used so routinely that some singers do not recognize their actual voices without it.

In this world of Instagram and Snapchat filters, where reality can be enhanced or distorted, people are seeking authenticity, including authentic leaders. One of my favorite examples of an authentic leader is my former colleague Barb Billhardt. Barb's superpower is that she cares deeply about people, and her caring is transparent. Barb ran HR at the division we worked in, and it was not always an easy job. As in any workplace, there were tensions, disputes, and unhappy people. In each instance, Barb treated everyone with respect and love.

At her current firm, during brutal cold weather featuring temperatures of –25 degrees Fahrenheit, some of Barb's colleagues had to come into the office to meet deadlines they had committed to on behalf of clients. Although Barb could have worked from home, she came into the office, made a point of thanking each person personally, and bought the employees lunch. Barb demonstrated her authenticity by showing up when she didn't have to, by thanking her people personally, and by feeding them.

Although HR is sometimes seen as the company's police force, Barb's approach inspires real trust between her and her colleagues. Barb's authenticity and caring for her colleagues makes her a trusted leader despite operating in a role that often inspires suspicion and mistrust.

Contrast Barb's example with that of Mary Beth, whose boss asked her to take on a third client. Mary Beth calculated she could work twenty-four hours a day and not have enough hours to take on the additional client. Despite pointing this out, her boss refused to change his mind. When she asked why, she was told it was because she was the only one on the team without three clients. Although the firm has identified Mary Beth as a rising star and invested in her with training and mentors, her inauthentic boss is driving her to consider leaving the firm. She is learning, painfully, that her boss doesn't really care about her.

Despite living in a filtered world where songs and photos can be endlessly manipulated to be "perfect," we all crave authenticity.

Leaders who are real stand out immediately as authentic.

We want to work with them and to be like them. We know that what we see in them is what we get. We know we can trust them.

We have the opportunity to care every day. When we demonstrate that our people matter, we are genuine and 100 percent real. In this Auto-Tune world, people can tell the difference.

And now you will have to excuse me, I need to learn how to remove filters on Instagram . . .

Your Favorite Banned Songs

While being given a tour of a performing arts school, I noticed a poster tacked up in a music classroom. The poster was titled "The List" and said, "Music no one needs to hear for a while. Thank you for not singing or playing these songs." The list had more than thirty songs, including vocal music, musical theater, and instrumentals. The songs on the list included "Hallelujah" (all versions), the complete works of Adele, "Somewhere Over the Rainbow," the complete works of Amy Winehouse, *Hairspray*, *Wicked*, *Les Miserables*, *Wii Music*, music from *Super Mario Brothers*, "Fur Elise" (unless it was all the parts), "Take on Me" by A Ha, and "Wonderwall" by Oasis.

The poster made me curious. Why would a music teacher ban these songs from a classroom? Wasn't this heavy-handed for a performing arts school? Weren't the students going to such a school to learn how to play and sing songs? My tour guide explained that upon starting at the school, many of the students only know how to play a handful of popular songs. During breaks between classes or for talent shows, they tend to play from their limited repertoire. The teacher created the list to force the students to go beyond their comfort songs and to learn new songs and grow.

We are not so different from the music students. We have our favorite tools, actions, and habits that we return to over and over again. We know them well, and it's easy to use them. When we do this too often, however, we become stuck and struggle.

My favorite tool for a long time was my poker face (apologies to Lady Gaga). Since childhood, I had concealed my emotions and feelings and became quite good at doing so. As a leader, my poker face was my default operating mode. While there were times when this was useful, I began to receive feedback that I was hard to read and made people uncomfortable. This was hard to hear because what I considered a strength was now being called out as a weakness. After reflecting on this, I realized people were saying, "We can't trust you if we can't read your feelings. Unless you don't have feelings . . ." Since then, I have been learning to play a new song called "Vulnerability," a song that includes opening up and sharing my feelings and thoughts with my colleagues. This has been quite difficult because I had thought being vulnerable was a weakness to be covered up or eliminated.

Looking back, I now see how limited I was in playing the poker face song over and over again. It created distance and uncertainty between my colleagues and me and kept me from developing a deeper level of trust.

We have our comfort zones and default modes. While they always have some value, the longer we use them, the more limited we become, like a musician who can play only a handful of songs.

Do you know what songs a music teacher would forbid you from playing? Do you know what songs you would benefit from learning? While on this journey to grow and learn, it's worth considering the answers to these questions. And now you will have to excuse me while I practice singing some Adele . . .

What I Learned at My Ninety-Day Off-Site

Dad deeply believed in learning. A lifelong learner who was intensely curious and an avid reader, he attempted to pass this on to his children with varying degrees of success. He also believed summer vacation was bad for kids because it took them away from the rhythms of learning. Out of this belief, he created what he called the "Summer Program." The program ran five days a week all summer and had two daily components: 1) a series of chores to be accomplished that day; and 2) a study program consisting of doing math problems as well as reading and summarizing articles he had torn out of the newspaper. When Dad got home from work, he would walk through the house with us, inspecting our chores, and later that night he would grade our Summer Program work.

The Summer Program created a shared experience for my siblings and me. It was something unique to our family and created a mutual cohesion and unity (though I use the word "unity" lightly about our highly competitive family). Many years later, after Dad had retired and had been traveling for several months, he returned home and said, "I'm selling the house. If any of you want anything, you should come and get it. Otherwise, I am throwing it away. And oh . . . I am leaving again, and I want you to clean up the house and get it ready for sale." For the next few weekends, my siblings and I went to Dad's house and readied it for sale. It was simply another version of the Summer Program. While it was not all sweetness and light amongst us as we worked on cleaning up the house, the mission was accomplished and his house was sold.

It is impossible to ignore the benefits of mutual unity and cohesion acquired through shared experiences. It can be as simple as a team project or an all-hands-on-deck crisis. These shared experiences force people to work together to achieve a common goal. As the team and business move forward, people get to know each other in new ways. These shared experiences stitch people together in a way that could never be accomplished at an off-site meeting or team-building exercise.

At one firm where I worked, the US mutual fund team forged extremely tight bonds after launching a start-up mutual fund business. Over the first three years, the business performed terribly, losing tens of millions of dollars. The team came under extreme pressure to raise assets or see the business shut down. To the credit of the team and our colleagues at headquarters in London, the business began experiencing "hockey stick" growth in year four, and the mutual fund business ultimately grew to be more than 10 percent of the firm's worldwide assets.

During the decade or so after the business began to grow, the mutual fund team successfully took on numerous challenges, in part based on their mutual trust and cohesion. This trust ran all the way to the CEO, who supported the business during the early, hard years.

> We should not neglect the opportunity to put teams together in a crucible that forges them for the future. These bonds can run for decades and form the cornerstone of a great culture.

Although I don't miss the Summer Program and I didn't do it with my kids, it taught me how a team receives long-term value from doing hard things together. And now you will excuse me; it's summertime, and I have some chores to do . . .

Going Stale

I know an impressive CEO named Greg who has done a great job after taking over a struggling firm. By reworking critical parts of the business and convincing a regulator to remove operating constraints, the business was enjoying its first profits in many years. In addition, shareholders had received their first ever dividend, and the business was now in the top 5 percent of its competitors.

After the adrenaline and buzz of fighting for survival, suddenly life was calmer. This new world felt strange to Greg. Without another tough challenge, he worried that he and the team might go stale. To keep the team engaged, Greg was tempted to begin a major project involving ripping out the firm's technology. But after reflecting on why he was attracted to the project, Greg realized he didn't know whether it was necessary. Did the business really need the new technology at this moment? Or was he simply looking to keep the team fresh? After seeing the technology project was more about keeping the team engaged, Greg put the project on hold. Freed from firefighting, he began working on a strategic plan to determine where to take the business. After eighteen months of crisis and chaos, Greg realized he and the team needed a breather as well as clarity about what was next.

When I was a kid, we had a breadbox in our kitchen. It was during a time when bread was made at home or sold at a bakery. Bread didn't have preservatives, nor did it come in a plastic bag, and therefore breadboxes were used to keep bread fresh. Breadboxes were so widespread that the game twenty questions included the question, "Is it bigger than a breadbox?" As it became easier to keep bread from going stale, breadboxes disappeared from the kitchen, and today they seem old-fashioned and quaint.

When we and the team are performing at a high level, we want to stay in that space. Looking for the equivalent of a breadbox, we can be seduced by the buzziness of busy. It can feel that by staying busy, we will stay fresh. How can we avoid this trap? One way is by reflecting the way the CEO did. After stepping back, he was able to see the technology project was like a breadbox, and he didn't actually know whether it was the most important thing for the team to work on.

Staying fresh is an ongoing challenge. In some instances, you can stay fresh by benchmarking yourself against other firms. In the CEO's case, he was aware of online competitors that offered an example for how the firm could evolve and change. This led him to realize his first priority was to create a strategic plan that would include comparing and contrasting the business to its online competitors.

Growing stale also happens when things are going well. Everything seems to work, and mistakes go unnoticed. Consider the real estate developer whose projects, while profitable, struggled with cost overruns. Each new project went over budget, often as a result of a sloppy and undisciplined construction team. A rising market saved the developer, however. As the market rose higher than he had anticipated, the sale prices of the projects more than offset the cost overruns. Seeing these profits, the construction team came to believe they were performing at a high level. In reality, they were simply the beneficiaries of a rising market. When the market stopped rising, the company endured a painful time and barely survived. By becoming stale and complacent during the good times, the company nearly went bankrupt.

While breadboxes are no longer required in kitchens, not growing stale is an ongoing challenge for us.

In good times and bad we have to work to learn new ways to see the world and ourselves.

And now will you excuse me while I make myself some delicious multigrain toast . . .

Seeing the
Small Things

A few years ago, while in the process of acquiring a historically significant building on behalf of a client, I went to visit the head of the local architectural preservation society. Assuming we were successful in acquiring the building, we were considering making some minor changes to the building's rear exterior, and I wanted to understand whether the preservation society would oppose these changes. The building was located in a large city, and the society's views carried a lot of influence. Before we got too far in our planning, we wanted to understand the society's thinking, and that was the reason for our meeting.

The meeting went well, and the head of the society said he thought our plans would be something they would support. He then suggested that we drive to the building and look at it together. He offered to drive, and soon we were winding our way through crowded city streets in his foreign sports car. While weaving around a double-parked car, the head of the society hit the side view mirror of the other car. Rather than stopping, he drove on and went into a tirade, blaming the owner of the other car for double-parking.

I was shocked. We had just damaged someone's car and hadn't stopped to make good on the minor damage. We drove on, and went and looked at the building where the society head confirmed he had no issues with our plans. I never saw or spoke to him again.

I occasionally think about our car ride and what I learned from it. I think about it from the perspective that small things can tell you big things. During that ride, I learned the head of the society had a bad temper and didn't accept responsibility for his actions. He didn't believe he was capable of making mistakes. I realized in that instant that he would be very difficult to work with and was glad he wasn't going to oppose our plans.

We often do small things that have a larger meaning. I had a boss who would inevitably start shuffling papers or looking at email when I went to meet with him. My feelings were hurt during these visits because his body language told me he wanted me out of his office. Over time, I realized that I represented an area of the business he didn't enjoy, and when I walked into his office, my very presence carried with it a long trail of problems and issues. It wasn't me he disliked; it was the business I was running. But it took me a long time to understand the message from his body language.

Conversely, I had a boss who always gave everyone his full and undivided attention when they came into his office. It was extremely powerful; he gave people the impression there was nothing more important in that moment than them.

Similarly, the people around you and on your team are sending messages with small acts and gestures. I recall that while touring a shopping mall with its property manager, the manager stopped, bent down, and picked up a piece of garbage. In that moment, he demonstrated to me he "owned" the mall. It was a small gesture that spoke volumes, and I saw the manager in a different light after that gesture.

We can be better leaders when we observe the small things that tell us large things.

So often we are distracted and not in the moment, and can miss these critical small things. Beginning with ourselves, we should be aware of our own small gestures while tuning in to small things around us. In the meantime, you will have to excuse me; I have to move my double-parked car . . .

Getting Out of the Way

On my leadership journey, I have had lots of humbling experiences but perhaps none so humbling as the day I learned I was no longer needed. Or at least needed in the way I wanted to be needed.

At the time, I was leading a group comprised of the heads of back-office business units. The group met weekly, and its purpose was to share information and create lines of communication between the unit heads. The group had been in existence for about a decade and always struggled to find cohesion. While the teams worked well independently, the group heads found it difficult to see why the group existed.

Perhaps it's more accurate to say that I struggled to find a way to bring them together in a way they found to be useful. I tried a lot of things: off-site meetings, team-wide goals, more independence and less independence. Nothing really worked. Then one day, two of the group heads approached about me about disbanding the group in favor of a series of committees. The committees would not only replace the old group but would include social, newsletter, and charitable committees. My first reaction was to say no. It was such a departure from our existing structure that I had difficulty accepting the proposal. But when I reflected on it, I realized my efforts had been a failure, and if the group had their own solution, the worst thing that could happen was another failure. Since it was the group's idea, it was likely they would work hard to make it successful.

I decided to think about the request as an A/B test. An A/B test is one where you compare two different versions of something to see which one is better. By thinking about the request as an opportunity to iterate and learn more about the best solution, I became more comfortable with the group self-managing itself. Still there was a part of me that was uneasy. Shouldn't I be doing something too?

I have written elsewhere about how much of the daily work we do doesn't really matter. Daily work may matter for technical or administrative reasons, but it isn't a game changer. And while a leader may work on three or four things a year that matter, it's often unclear in the moment what those three or four things are. How can we know where to really focus as if our hair were on fire?

The A/B committee test proved to be a spectacular success. Freed to do things as they saw fit, what had been a reluctant group became a series of high performing, self-managing teams. Working together in new ways that were soon the talk of the firm, the committee's success was later emulated in other regions around the world. More importantly, the committees became the vehicles where people worked on improving and refining our culture.

In hindsight, the committees turned out to be one of the three or four things that really mattered during that year. It was also humbling: all that was required of me was to say yes and get out of the way (thank you, Kris and Dustin!). Although it feels wrong, sometimes the best thing we can do is stay out of the way. And now you will excuse me while I figure out those three or four things that matter . . .

Tickets and Triggers

Michelle and I both received traffic tickets over a two-week period. Our different responses to those tickets illustrate something we encounter over and over again in our lives.

I received my ticket on the outskirts of Cleveland. Passing a police car on the side of the road, I saw I was seven miles over the speed limit. "I am okay," I thought. "Barely over the speed limit."

When the officer pulled out, switched on his lights, and then came up behind me, I was perplexed. It couldn't be me. But it was. It turned out I had missed a sign showing the speed limit dropped by ten miles per hour. I was driving seventeen miles over the speed limit, not seven.

Although I was chagrined to receive the ticket, I was speeding. The ticket was a consequence of my actions, and all I could do was accept it and pay it. In the past, I have received tickets I thought were "unfair" and had a far different response where I felt victimized.

Michelle received her ticket for not coming to a complete stop before making a right turn at a red light. The ticket came in the mail and included a picture of her car at the intersection. Because the picture showed her brake lights were engaged, Michelle believed she had come to a complete stop and the "unfair" ticket triggered her sense of injustice.

Our reactions are examples of what happens when we are triggered or not triggered by outside events. We all have triggers. They might be someone "backseat driving," people who are late, or someone who does not clean up the kitchen after a meal. Michelle and I have come to understand that one of our triggers is an "injustice" trigger. An injustice trigger means we become upset when we feel like victims of injustice. Receiving a ticket we don't believe we deserve is an example of an injustice trigger.

We see and experience triggers all the time. We have our own triggers, and those around us have their triggers as well.

Triggers are challenging because they often set off an outsized response that becomes worse than the triggering event. For example, the rare shouting matches I had in my career occurred when I was triggered. Indignant and offended that someone thought I was harming him or her, I lost my temper. At the time I didn't understand the concept of being triggered; I just knew I was being wrongly accused and lost my temper as a result. In other words, I had been driving within the speed limit but received a ticket.

We need to understand the things that trigger us and work on ourselves to minimize our responses to them. We also need to be aware that those around us have triggers. When we trigger someone and receive an outsized response, we need to work to minimize our response. This is not easy. When my injustice trigger gets tripped, it's difficult not to become upset. If I can recognize, however, that I am being triggered, I can work to respond differently.

Triggers are often the result of innocent or unconscious behaviors.

I saw this happen while working at a company that had been acquired by another company. During the integration phase with the new company, one of my colleagues from the old company frequently referred to processes and procedures that had been in place at our prior company. He would use the name of the prior company by saying things like, "When we were at XYZ, we did it this way." By using the name of the prior company, he triggered our new colleagues. For them, using the name of the other company felt as if they were being told their way was the wrong way. Had my colleague been sensitive to this, he might have framed his comments differently by saying something like, "I have seen it done in this way," or "Have you ever considered this approach?"

Triggers are part of our personal and professional lives. We can be more effective when we recognize our own triggers and control them. We can also be more effective by recognizing them in others. And now you will excuse me while I drive Michelle to contest her speeding ticket . . .

Solo Jumping

Sometimes Michelle and I find ourselves in a conversational cul-de-sac, where neither of us understands what the other is talking about. In observing how we arrive at these confusing conversations, I have come to realize that she and I are both "jumpers." By "jumpers" I mean we abruptly jump from one topic to another without a transition. We will be speaking about one subject, and that topic will trigger a completely unrelated but important thought. Without bringing the other person along or saying something like "that reminds me" or "unrelated to what we are talking about," we jump to the next topic. Because the other person is still on the first topic, they don't make the jump. This usually results in a conversation where one of us says, "I have no idea what you are talking about," or tries unsuccessfully to make the jump but lands in the wrong location. Immersed in our own logic, we often become irritated that the other person hasn't kept up with what seems perfectly obvious to us.

For example, today we were having a conversation about how our run had gone. Discussing the run led me to think about the bad weather predicted during the next few days, which reminded me we were traveling for the next few days. Thinking about the trip reminded me I had cancelled a doctor's appointment on the day we were returning home in case bad weather would delay us. So when I said "oh by the way, I cancelled my doctor's appointment on Monday," it made perfect sense to me. Michelle, however, was still back on our original subject and was confused what my doctor's appointment had to do with today's run. She then tried to make the jump into Monday and landed on another subject, leaving us both confused and irritated. This was entirely my fault. I had jumped without her and failed to understand I was jumping solo.

We can find we are jumping all the time. We focus intently on an issue and forget that everyone else is working on other things and not in lockstep with us. Or we go back and revisit a subject from fifteen minutes ago, and everyone else thinks we are talking about the current subject.

Solo jumping can occur in all sorts of ways. I am an avid reader and enjoy sharing articles with my colleagues. On more than one occasion, an article I sent to the team with an "FYI" attached to it caused people to reach conclusions I could have never contemplated. I had jumped without them and caused confusion or paranoia by failing to bring them along.

In another case, a leader was asked by her team to respond to a business plan. Intending to give them more detail later when she had the time, she responded with a single sentence that was nothing more than a passing thought. Assuming this was her full response, her team spent a considerable time working on what they thought she was asking of them. It was only later that the leader and her team found they had both jumped solo.

Ideally, we should seek to
jump in tandem.

Tandem jumping requires thinking about the
other person, understanding their perspective, and
testing to make sure they understand us. When we
do this, we avoid confusion and errors that are easily
avoided. And now you will have to excuse me; I have
to go tell Michelle something right now . . .

Comfortably Numb

It's only human to go numb. We go numb to the Post-it left on the fridge seven months ago, the crack in the sidewalk, or that spot of peeling paint on the wall. Art thieves targeting an art gallery have been known to repeatedly set off a burglar alarm over a long weekend. After responding multiple times and finding nothing wrong, the police and employees stop investigating, thereby leaving the thieves free to enter and steal valuable paintings.

During my career I was asked to temporarily take over the IT department of a large real estate company. The assignment was meant to last a month and instead lasted a year. I learned a lot from my time there, including the challenge of hearing alarm bells.

The company's IT systems ran on a mainframe, which was housed in a glass box that had a dedicated thermostat for keeping the glass box at a cool temperature. Some of the IT staff were responsible for the care of the mainframe and took turns carrying a pager that would call them if the temperature in the room became too warm. During a week in June, the pager began going off for reasons no one could understand; the temperature in the room was appropriate and everything seemed fine. The following weekend, the pager began calling the staff member who was on call for mainframe problems. Assuming the calls were related to the earlier false alarms, he turned off his pager. On Sunday evening we noticed the company's IT systems were down and discovered the mainframe room had become so hot that the mainframe had shut itself down.

I now had a full-blown crisis. Without the mainframe back up and running, no one would be able to use his or her computers on Monday morning. This meant little work would be done, including collecting and depositing rents. I also had no idea whether the heat had irreparably damaged the mainframe. If it had, it meant our systems might be down for days or weeks. I also had no idea what had caused the mainframe to overheat. Finally, I had to tell the CEO and senior team the terrible story about why the team had ignored the alarms. I could just hear their responses: "So the person carrying the pager ignored the pages? Why haven't you fired them?" "What kind of people do you have down there?"

To add to the crisis, the Chicago Bulls were playing in Chicago in the NBA championship game. If they won the game being played that evening, they would win the championship. It also meant the police might close off the downtown to prevent damage by vandals. If the access to the downtown was closed, we might not be able to get to our building and repair the mainframe.

In the end, I was quite fortunate. Despite the Bulls winning the championship, a technician was able to get downtown on Sunday evening. He brought the mainframe back up and pronounced it undamaged. We also discovered that fluff (seeds) from cottonwood trees had clogged the mainframe's dedicated air conditioning system, causing it to fail. When the air conditioning failed, the heat from the mainframe caused the room to become too warm and the mainframe shut itself down. Having grown numb to the earlier false alarms, the on-call staff member ignored the texts he received as the mainframe began overheating.

I was relieved but realized how lucky I had been. While many things had gone wrong to bring about the crisis, the undamaged main frame was the result of many things going right. I kept thinking about how the CEO, who was famous for his short temper and knee-jerk reactions, would have responded. In all likelihood he would have fired me. Looking back across the years, putting myself back in the shoes of a younger Jim, I can still feel all the stress and fear.

The mainframe's meltdown taught me a lesson about paying closer attention to alarms. These alarms can be from a pager, or they can be the small voice we hear in our heads. Sometimes our voice keeps telling us something is wrong, and we keep ignoring it. We are too busy or we tell ourselves we will come back to it later. Sometimes our procrastination results in a crisis like the one I faced with the mainframe.

As humans, we like patterns and we like rhythms. They comfort us and make us feel safe. Our small voices, however, are like little alarms saying something may be wrong. Our little voices come for free, require no upkeep or training, and are one of the most powerful tools we have available to us.

By paying attention to our small voices, we can react before a crisis becomes full-blown.

Yes, it can feel fun to be solving a crisis. It feels better, however, to have a quiet weekend. And now you will have to excuse me while I answer my pager . . .

Squirrel!

Michelle came home from having coffee with her friend Kathy, and I asked how it had gone.

"Oh, it was great. We both say 'squirrel,' and then we're on to the next subject," she said.

Michelle was referring to her beloved Weimaraner, Comet. If someone said "Squirrel" to Comet, she would immediately become distracted and run to a window, barking and looking for a squirrel.

It's tempting to run to the window when someone yells "Squirrel." If we are bored, it can be fun to take on the new challenge the squirrel brings us.

> Sometimes we chase after a squirrel because the issues we are already facing are hard and it's easier to push them aside rather than deal with them.

Squirrels come in many forms and include anything that distracts us. My own squirrels are "knowledge emails." An email full of data, insights, or links to recommended books will get my attention. To overcome this, I put these emails into a "Reading" folder to be read later. By avoiding these squirrels, I can stay focused on my critical work.

Squirrels also come in the form of people. Some people have a talent for delegating up. Delegating up means giving your boss your problem and asking them to solve it. When we are in squirrel mode, we jump at anything, even things that are not our problem. Beyond distracting ourselves, taking the other person's problem prevents them from growing by wrestling with it themselves. If we do this frequently enough, we find we are doing the jobs of two or more people.

Sometimes the squirrel will be a new product or initiative. At one firm I worked at, we were faced with a competing product that was receiving a lot of publicity but not a lot of sales. Our firm (and nearly all our competitors) had previously missed out on the explosive growth of a similar product, and we wanted to avoid making the same mistake again. We found ourselves at a classic point where it was unclear what we should do. Should we invest a lot of time and money to avoid being left behind? But what if the new product was a bust in the market? Should we wait until it was clear the new product was going to enjoy customer demand? After a lot of debate, we decided to be a "fast follower." Being a fast follower meant we would wait to see how and whether a market developed for the product. If a market did develop, we would then quickly follow with our own version of the product.

We arrived at this decision because we had limited resources and weren't convinced the product would succeed. Despite pressure to launch our own version of the product, we regularly revisited our decision and saw no growth requiring us to move as a fast follower.

Five years later, the product, while continuing to offer much promise, has yet to find customers. By choosing a fast follower strategy, we avoided the squirrel trap.

Squirrels are a daily challenge. They can be emails, texts, or decisions to launch new products. Squirrels are only avoided by asking, "What outcome am I seeking, and does working on this help me achieve that outcome?" While it can be fun to chase squirrels like Comet did, we risk exhausting ourselves and making no progress on critical work. And now you will excuse me while I go peek at the backyard; I think I see a squirrel . . .

Ego, Anger, and Road Rage

Last week, while walking through our neighborhood, Michelle and I witnessed a strange and curious instance of road rage. Walking north on Forest Avenue, a quiet residential street, we were on the last block before Forest ends at Ogden Avenue. Ogden is a busy four-lane road that sees thirty-five thousand cars a day as it passes through our town. Entering Ogden from any residential street, including Forest, is nerve-wracking because it is difficult to find a gap in traffic, particularly if you wish to make a left turn against traffic.

There were two cars stopped at the intersection, the first car, seeking to make a left turn. Our attention was called to the two cars when the second car began beeping impatiently at the first car. The driver of the first car, a middle-aged man, got out of his car, walked back to the second car, and began yelling at the driver, who was a young woman. We couldn't hear what was being said, but the man's body language was one of anger mixed with frustration, sort of an exasperated "what do you expect me to do?"

The man returned to his car and waited again for a break in traffic. To our surprise, the woman pulled alongside the man on his left side, effectively blocking any Ogden traffic from entering Forest Avenue. Suddenly, she darted left into traffic, threading an impossibly small gap in traffic, and was gone from sight.

I was stunned. By pulling alongside the first car and blocking any traffic turning from Ogden, she risked a head-on collision or creating a pile-up crash. In addition, by darting out into traffic, she risked causing a multi-car accident. Of course, she had made her point: it was indeed possible to make a left turn onto Ogden in heavy traffic—that is, so long as you were willing to risk your life and the lives of others.

The incident caused me to reflect on how ego, anger, and impatience affects us. Impatience is an easy street to drive on as a leader. There is so much pressure for results, for responses, and for activity that being impatient can feel comfortable. Waiting for anything, including a break in traffic, becomes intolerable, and we find ourselves acting because we are always acting, always doing something.

Regarding ego, Marshall Goldsmith points out that the overriding need to be right is one of the reasons we fail in our roles. I have certainly suffered from this and continue to struggle with it. I still cringe thinking about correcting a colleague when they were telling a story and mixed up San Diego and Seattle. It had no bearing on the outcome of the story, yet I was unable to help myself from jumping in and correcting them. Not only did I break the rhythm of his story, but I made my colleague feel persecuted. And to what end? To show I knew the difference between San Diego and Seattle? The young woman driver showed the other driver she was right, but it could have come at a horrible cost.

Driven by the overriding need to be right, our egos can be terribly damaging to our teams and to us.

Anger is another challenge for us. It blocks our ability to think and act effectively and can cause long-lasting harm. I recall having a shouting match with a colleague because I was triggered when I felt falsely accused. It was a bad response on my part and took a lot of work to repair. Presumably the young woman driver was angry after being shouted at by the other driver and made a rash decision. It's tempting to look at what the young woman did and be critical of her actions. If I am honest, however, who among us hasn't acted in anger? The woman's actions serve as a useful reminder for me to reflect on how I can improve my responses when I am triggered.

Seeing the road rage and reflecting upon it caused me to reflect that I too have acted out of impatience, ego, and anger. There will always be busy streets with unbroken streams of traffic. The challenge is in being open to the alternatives. When I head to Ogden, I take a slower road with a stoplight that allows me to turn onto Ogden without undue stress. And now you will excuse me; someone behind me is beeping their horn . . .

The Toughest Puzzle

Michelle and I and some of our kids enjoy watching the reality TV show *Survivor*. The show's premise is that twenty people are stranded on an island and play to win $1 million. The contestants are formed into two or three tribes, given very little to eat, and compete to win food and immunity challenges. The tribe that wins a food challenge receives a feast that helps offset their starvation diets. A team that loses an immunity challenge must turn on each other and vote off one of its members. Eventually only three or four contestants remain, and a jury comprised of tribe members who were voted off earlier chooses the winning contestant.

The food and immunity challenges often feature a grueling physical challenge coupled with solving a puzzle. Puzzles are a consistent portion of the challenges, and frequently the difference between winning and losing a challenge comes down to how quickly the tired and hungry contestants can solve a puzzle.

We often discuss whether we would want to compete on *Survivor*, and, if so, what the hardest parts of the experience would be. For me, because I am a poor swimmer, the water challenges would be a struggle, as would solving puzzles.

Puzzles confound me. I have a difficult time seeing how pieces might fit together, and I certainly would be challenged to do one quickly. Over Christmas, some of the kids completed a one-thousand-piece puzzle, and I was very impressed; their patience, teamwork, and ability to sort out the pieces was quite good.

Daily, we face puzzles from the people we work with. We are all complicated and contradictory beings. Often, the face we wear to work is different from who we really are. We all have different ambitions and desires, many of which we do not articulate. Solving people puzzles is an ongoing challenge and one of the most important challenges we face.

One of the best things we can do when working on people puzzles is to shut off our minds and pay attention to body language. Shutting off your mind means not thinking about what you are going to say while the other person is talking. It means listening deeply while looking out for clues in what the other person is saying.

Often, the biggest clues are in their body language.

We tend to ignore body language because we are either thinking about what we are going to say next or focusing solely on words.

Body language can be quite illuminating. At my kick-off meeting with a coaching client named Dan, I watched him shielding his face and doodling while his boss was speaking. When Dan later told me that he had a poor relationship with his boss, I wasn't surprised.

It takes real work to pay attention to body language. We are so used to being in our own heads that concentrating on another person is work. For example, just putting away our phones and focusing on the other person can take real effort. Yet one of our greatest accomplishments is solving the puzzle of who someone else is. When we have a deep understanding of the others around us, we can be more effective and more connected. Contestants on *Survivor* might do ten or so puzzles over the course of the season. Over a forty-year career, we will have the opportunity to solve hundreds of people puzzles. And now you will excuse me while I turn on the TV; *Survivor* is starting . . .

One Thing Every Leader Should Do

There are just a handful of things I wish I knew earlier in my career. Avoiding the meeting after the meeting is one of those things.

My insight came while I was sitting at a coffee shop and doing some work. I was sitting between two tables, and at each table were two people who were obviously coworkers. The people at each table were discussing other people they work with. While their conversations weren't overly negative, they were also unlikely to be shared with the people they were discussing.

Later, it struck me I had heard what some people call "the meeting after the meeting" or the MATM. The MATM occurs when people don't speak up during a meeting and then reconvene in a smaller group to discuss the meeting and share their real thoughts. The MATM is part of a low-trust culture where people don't feel comfortable being candid. In thinking about the conversations I overheard, I realized how much time and brainpower is wasted within companies as a result of the MATM.

The constant need for reassurance is also a feature of a MATM culture. If you and I have a conversation criticizing a third person, it's likely that after our meeting is over, you will begin wondering whether I will have a conversation with someone else where we criticize you. In other words, if I am someone who criticizes people behind their backs, isn't it likely I might criticize you behind your back? To make sure I am not criticizing you in private, you then feel the need to talk to others who might speak with me and learn what I might have been saying about you. All this checking in takes a lot of time and attention. And none of this is in our job descriptions or helps grow the business.

This is an area where we can make a difference. By not engaging in MATM discussions, we can set the tone. When someone wants to gossip or grumble about a third party, we can call it out and ask for their help in creating a culture without MATMs. We can push for frank discussions in a meeting and ask for input from people who are not speaking up.

There are a million things outside our control. We do control, however, how we expect our team to act with each other and with us. We also control how we respond to our team when they want to engage in MATMs. Looking back, I see how I was part of the MATM problem. If I had understood it at the time, I might have been able to avoid doing it and have been a more effective leader. And now you will excuse me while I get some more coffee . . .

Taking Shortcuts

When I was a kid, one of my great joys was finding a shortcut. There were lots of alleys and gangways in our neighborhood, and I could slip out of sight and appear somewhere else, almost as if by magic. Shortcuts were special because it seemed as if no one else knew about them and they offered me a way to get somewhere more quickly.

As an adult I also enjoy taking shortcuts. While running with my brother Kevin, I dashed through a stranger's backyard on Thanksgiving in an effort to beat him home (he spotted me taking the shortcut, so it didn't work out).

Shortcuts are useful, and we all use them, perhaps more than we realize. For example, speeding drivers slow down when it appears there is a police car on the side of the road ahead of them. They know from past experience that police cars park in certain places for the purpose of giving speeding drivers a ticket. The speeding driver who slows down does not actually know whether a police car is up ahead. Instead, using the shape of the car and its location, they take a mental shortcut to make a quick decision.

Our two Yorkies, Marley and Emmy, also use shortcuts when they bark at the monsters displayed on lawns during Halloween. Seeing a vague, sinister figure on a lawn, they react without taking the time to verify whether the figure is dangerous or even a human.

Some companies are in the business of providing shortcuts. The mutual fund ranking service, Morningstar, ranks mutual funds from one star (the worst) to five stars (the best). For investors lacking the time or acumen to assess the performance of thousands of mutual funds, Morningstar's rankings offer a useful shortcut. Yelp and TripAdvisor are other examples of shortcuts for those looking for reliable restaurant or hotel recommendations.

Whether we know it or not, we are no different from speeders or Yorkies. Using shortcuts helps us make faster decisions when looking at data or during a meeting when receiving customer feedback. Shortcuts are most effective when we know the subject well, or when we are making low-risk decisions or decisions that can be quickly revised in the face of more data.

While it feels satisfying to get somewhere quickly, sometimes taking a shortcut brings the wrong result. For mutual fund investors, blindly buying the highest rated fund can mean buying just when performance is peaking. Or sometimes those investors naively rely on crowd-sourced recommendations that can be manipulated by customers with a grudge or by owners seeking to artificially improve their ratings.

We should employ shortcuts thoughtfully.

When we use the last month of someone's performance as the basis for an annual review, we are using what we easily recall rather than doing the heavy lifting of considering the entire twelve months. This can result in a performance review that is too rosy or too harsh.

To use shortcuts is human. We should reflect on their use, seeking to use them to our advantage while avoiding ones that can lead to poor outcomes. And now you will have to excuse me while I work out a new shortcut to beat Kevin . . .

Embracing
the Suck

During my late thirties, I received a big promotion.
I was transferred to a new division where I suddenly
found myself with lots of challenges. The person I
replaced had been let go and was suing the company.
I was deposed as part of the lawsuit and found it to
be a stressful experience. The team I was now leading
was upset because they believed a member of the
team should have received my job. They were polite,
but cold. Shortly after I started the new job, a big
customer fired us. After the high of being promoted,
suddenly nothing was going well. Looking back now,
I see how much I was shaped as a leader during that
time. While painful, all these challenges brought me
to a better place as I learned about leading a team
during a difficult period.

Last summer, Michelle and I toured a small
vineyard in Napa Valley called Brown Estate. Over
several decades the owners had reworked the property
from an abandoned farm to a vineyard. We chanced
to meet the winemaker, David Brown, at the end
of our tour and chatted with him. With just a few
weeks before harvest, I asked what was keeping him
up at night. "Everything," he said. "Dry rot, fires,

temperature . . ." He went on to say that the years when nothing goes wrong are often the years that produce lackluster vintages.

David's insight that challenging conditions produce the best wines intrigued me and led me to consider how this might apply to the broader world. It might mean that the "easy" days are the ones to be most concerned about. Is complacency creeping in? Or is the business operating so well that it is vulnerable to disruption? Nokia and BlackBerry are examples of once dominant firms that were disrupted while at the top.

The same might also apply to us. Could we learn to look at the "hard" days as ones to be embraced in the belief they produce the best of who we are? There is a military saying, "Embrace the Suck," which embodies this concept. This is counterintuitive, as embracing hard things goes against our nature. We all would rather have a placid, serene day where everything goes according to plan. When I think back about the challenges I have faced as a leader, however, what made me better as a human and as a businessperson were the hard things. David's insight helps me see the hard times in a new light.

Embracing the Suck is not easy in the moment when we find ourselves wrestling with problems in the middle of the night. These are the hard, difficult things with no easy solutions. They are also the things that form and shape us for future challenges. As much as we want to avoid them, the hard things create the best vintages, be it for wine or for leaders. And now you will excuse while I go drink some of David's excellent zinfandel (which definitely doesn't suck) . . .

It's Always about Me. It's Never about Me.

It's never about me, and it's always about me. Let me explain. A few weeks ago, Phil, the division head of a large company, was trying to reach me. A mutual friend got in touch and asked how Phil could connect with me. We agreed Phil would call me later that week.

"What could it be about?" I wondered. Maybe he wanted to offer me a job or get my insights on a big project. In the time leading up to the call, I thought about it. A lot. Each time I thought about it, I thought about how it related to me. It felt good to be needed even if I didn't know exactly for what. Given the urgency around setting up our call, it must be something big and important.

Finally, the phone rang, and after a few pleasantries, Phil got to why he was calling. His company had invested in a business, the investment wasn't performing as forecast, and there was tension and disagreement between his company and the business they had invested in. Phil was meeting with the CEO of the other business to discuss the things that were not going well. Phil remembered that the

CEO and I had been on a board together, and he wanted to pick my brain about the CEO ahead of the meeting.

Oh. The call wasn't about me. It was about Phil and the problems in his world. I had spent countless times in my head thinking about me when I should have been thinking about Phil. Had I been able to put myself in his shoes, I would have immediately understood why he wanted to speak with me.

Although the call was bruising to my ego, it was a wonderful reminder that it's never about me. It's always about the other person. What I mean is that we all have self-interest. We spend all day thinking about what we want and how to get it. Had I been able to remember this, I would have been prepared for the call and not spent a lot of time thinking about myself.

This is one of the central challenges of leadership. We know what we want, and our success depends on getting what we want. Yet we can't get what we want unless we first understand what everyone else wants. Often, it's different from what we want. Unless we take the time to put ourselves in others' shoes and consider their self-interest, we run the risk of thinking only about ourselves.

When we think only about ourselves, we make it more difficult to succeed.

How do we enter someone else's shoes? It starts with the simple act of thinking, if you were them, what would you want? This forces you to think about their self-interest and compare it to your own. The next step is just as important: ask them questions to try and understand their self-interest. Why? One reason is it's easier to be told what someone wants than to guess at it. Another reason is sometimes our tunnel vision clouds our ability to see the other person accurately. When this happens, we can never see their self-interest. Finally, we often assume everyone wants what we want. When this is not the case, we both become frustrated.

And now you will have to excuse me; I have an important call coming in . . .

Last-Place Hero

In a prior life, Michelle lived next door to Jill and Bob. Balding and sporting a big beard long before it was trendy, Bob had heart disease and lived with it for a long time. His passions in life were running, drinking beer, and cutting down trees. And cutting down trees was a distant third in his priorities. Bob refused to let his heart condition interfere with running, and he ran races of different distances, including marathons. Sometimes Michelle and I would see him on a local running trail and wave or stop for a minute and chat. The way Bob lived life on his own terms, running through the woods despite his heart condition, was something I admired.

Bob died too young when he suffered a heart attack while running alone. He left a hole in our little world, and sometimes coming around a bend on the running trail, I half expect to see him running toward me. Two years ago, when I ran my first one-hundred-mile race, I carried Bob's funeral-mass card with me and held it up as I ran across the finish line. It was my way of saying he lived on within us.

Gone, yes.

Forgotten, no.

After suffering a virus that damaged her heart, Jill needed a pacemaker. Following Bob's lead, Jill took up running and she and Bob ran many races together. They also joined a running club called the Run to Eat Club, where they made lifelong friends.

Jill's heart and pacemaker require her to run at a sedate pace, something she finds frustrating. As her doctor told her, however, "Would you prefer to run faster or have a working heart?"

Limited to the pace her heart permits, Jill is often the last runner to finish a race. I frequently think about Jill's journey during a race and find it inspiring. She runs the race that has been marked out for her and does the best she can in her circumstances. It takes courage to keep going the way Jill does and requires tremendous mental strength. For all these reasons, Jill is one of my heroes.

While having dinner, Michelle and Jill discussed running. Jill spoke about being frustrated at finishing last during races. Michelle responded by telling Jill how she is one of my heroes. Jill was taken aback. She had no idea I felt this way and never thought she could be inspiring to others.

We can learn from Jill's perspective. Too often we get caught up in our own narrative and how we perceive ourselves.

> We can miss how our behavior impacts others, for better or for worse.

I serve on the board of a private company, and earlier this year a new member joined the board. She is quite accomplished, and the company is better for her insights and thinking. To be honest, I was a bit intimidated by her because she is so bright and has been so successful. After our last board meeting, she came up and told me how much she appreciated my comments and how much she learns from them. I was astounded. Like Jill, I had gotten stuck in my own narrative, telling myself that nothing I could say would be of value to the new board member.

We sometimes tell ourselves stories that miss the positive impact we have on others. So next time you are wondering if you are making a difference, remember that a line connects you and I back to Jill. And now you will excuse me while I check on the status of my Run to Eat Club application . . .

Conclusion

One Friday, I found out I was being temporarily assigned to run the IT department of a thousand-person company. The head of the department had just been fired, and I was to run it until his replacement could be found. The department was in chaos and poorly regarded by the rest of the company. I had no IT experience, and I didn't even work in the same building as the IT team. I went home in a panic. It seemed I was destined to fail and have a lot of stress along the way. The next day I went to a bookstore and bought a thick book about managing IT departments, and tried to finish reading it before Monday (I didn't). It wasn't that helpful, but it made me feel less stupid.

The assignment lasted about a year and went well. I made mistakes but also figured out how to fix the worst of the problems in the department. I figured out what to do by always coming back to the people. Focusing on the people in the department and focusing on the people in the rest of the company— the customers—led to finding a way out of the worst of the issues.

Focusing on the people sounds easy, but it is not. We are complex, complicated, and contradictory creatures. Therefore, so is leadership. What works today might not work tomorrow. Our journey as leaders is to keep evolving and growing so we can meet the challenges we face on a daily basis.

I hope this book has been helpful in your journey as a leader, and has given you some insights on what to do and what not to do as you go forward.

As part of my own journey, I am doing coaching, consulting, and speaking. I am happy to speak with you and give you my thoughts (at no charge) if you are considering working with me. I am also happy to hear about your own journey as a leader. You can reach me at jimobrien441@gmail.com. I look forward to hearing from you!

Acknowledgments

This book would not have been possible without the support from my friends and colleagues—people like Suzanne Cullinane, Barb Bilhardt, George Georgiev, Erika Oquist, Steph Pokuta, Dave Carpo, and Jess Hylander, who have so much yet to accomplish and who are on the Way. It has been a privilege to work with you, and I hope this book will be useful for you on your own journeys.

I have been blessed on my journey to work with a talented group of colleagues, including those at JMB Realty, Heitman, and Henderson Global Investors. You were more than patient with me (beginning with Denise Sliwinski!), and I am grateful to have worked with you. I grew and learned from your wisdom and counsel, and I am better for having known you. A special thanks to Karen Sheehan who always made my work better, to Graham Kitchen for teaching me the power of good questions, and to my "Domfather" Dom Cottone for his wisdom and counsel. I also learned much at the Stagen Leadership Academy, and I want to thank my classmates as well as my teachers Lisa Martin, Cindy Pladziewicz, and Raff Viton.

I want to thank David Emerald Womeldorff for graciously agreeing to write the foreword to this book. His book *The Power of TED** made an indelible impression on me and made me a better person. It is simply a dream come true to have David write the foreword. To the Creator in you, David!

I have felt like an impostor writing this book. It is the product of much prodding and encouragement, and it would not have been possible without first the suggestion of Bobby Chatterjee, the encouragement of Kathy D'Amore, all the help of all the good people at Round Table Companies including my amazing editor James Cook, and finally my wife Michelle who read every word and has been my biggest fan and cheerleader. Thank you all.

About the Author

Jim O'Brien has worked in senior roles for a variety of asset management organizations, including London-based Henderson Global Investors, where he was a member of the executive committee and oversaw its US business for nine years.

Jim served as a trustee of the Henderson Global Funds board and as president of Henderson Global Funds, and he was a board member of THRE, a $20 billion joint venture between TIAA-CREF and Henderson. Jim also served as a board member of The Olson Company, a California-based homebuilder.

Jim enjoys reading, gardening, and ultramarathons as well as spending time with his wife, Michelle, and their children.